Cambridge Elements

Elements in Metaphysics
edited by
Tuomas E. Tahko
University of Bristol

ONTOLOGICAL CATEGORIES

A Methodological Guide

Katarina Perović
University of Iowa

Shaftesbury Road, Cambridge CB2 8EA, United Kingdom

One Liberty Plaza, 20th Floor, New York, NY 10006, USA

477 Williamstown Road, Port Melbourne, VIC 3207, Australia

314–321, 3rd Floor, Plot 3, Splendor Forum, Jasola District Centre, New Delhi – 110025, India

103 Penang Road, #05–06/07, Visioncrest Commercial, Singapore 238467

Cambridge University Press is part of Cambridge University Press & Assessment, a department of the University of Cambridge.

We share the University's mission to contribute to society through the pursuit of education, learning and research at the highest international levels of excellence.

www.cambridge.org
Information on this title: www.cambridge.org/9781009475679

DOI: 10.1017/9781108973861

First published 2024

A catalogue record for this publication is available from the British Library

ISBN 978-1-009-47567-9 Hardback
ISBN 978-1-108-97825-5 Paperback
ISSN 2633-9862 (online)
ISSN 2633-9854 (print)

Ontological Categories

A Methodological Guide

Elements in Metaphysics

DOI: 10.1017/9781108973861
First published online: January 2024

Katarina Perović
University of Iowa

Author for correspondence: Katarina Perović, katarina-perovic@uiowa.edu

Abstract: Ontology – the study of the most fundamental categories of being – lies at the very heart of metaphysics. The reason why it appears to be so central is because it takes on the following questions: What sorts of entities are there? What features do those entities have? How do they relate to one another? And so on. Section 1 of this Element presents a fast-paced historical overview of some of the notable approaches to these questions. Section 2 tells the story of how one of the oldest, most disputed, but also most developed ontological categories – universals – got introduced. Section 3 builds on the discussion of universals as it considers the desiderata for a promising system of ontological categories. And Section 4 looks at ways in which philosophers might break with tradition and explore some new ontological categories.

This Element also has a video abstract: www.cambridge.org/Perović

Keywords: ontology, categories, entities, metaphysics, universals

ISBNs: 9781009475679 (HB), 9781108978255 (PB), 9781108973861 (OC)
ISSNs: 2633-9862 (online), 2633-9854 (print)

Contents

Introduction

Ontology – the study of the most fundamental categories of being – lies at the very heart of metaphysics. The reason why it appears to be so central is because it takes on the following questions: What sorts of entities are there? What features do those entities have? How do they relate to one another? And so on. The first question is both general and assuming. It is general in a sense that is not to be answered by listing all the things that one can think of, for it asks about the *sorts of entities* that there are, not just the sheer number of them. It is also an assuming question insofar as it takes for granted that the world is not empty but filled with entities and that these entities *can* in fact be categorized by appeal to their distinctive features and roles.

So how might one go about addressing such vast questions concerning the categories of being? In Section 1, I present a fast-paced historical overview of some of the notable approaches. I start with the naïve linguistic realism of Plato and Aristotle, who took natural language to be a reliable guide to the fundamental categories of being. Then I briefly discuss the three main skeptical attitudes to this form of ontological realism – Kantian skepticism, which questions whether the categories of being are indeed part of the structure of the world or merely part of our conceptual framework; skepticism about the types and numbers of categories; and skepticism about natural language as a guide to what there is. These forms of skepticism are still very much alive in contemporary approaches to metaphysics, as is the ontological realism that resists them.

Section 2 tells the story of how one of the oldest, most disputed, but also most developed ontological categories – universals – got introduced. I present the famous "one-over-many" argument for universals, as the argument was presented by Plato and then picked up and amplified by Aristotle. The goal of the section is to illustrate, through a case study of universals, what making a case for a category looks like, as well as to show the points at which other philosophers might disagree. One of the most prominent contemporary realists about universals – David Armstrong –believed that his version of "one over many" only offered a "preliminary case" for universals, not a decisive one. Building on this preliminary case, he added further arguments – the argument from laws of nature and the so-called negative arguments from Russell against the denial of relational universals; and from Pap and Jackson, from the lack of adequate paraphrases of apparent references to universals. In this way, Armstrong believed himself to be making a more convincing, cumulative, case for universals.

In Section 3, I draw on the example of the category of universals from Section 2 as I discuss the methodological desiderata for building a promising system of ontological categories. The first desideratum is to make sure that the metaphysical question or problem that the ontological entity is introduced to address is well-stated and motivated. This requires taking special care to avoid engaging with metaphysical pseudo-problems. I understand a metaphysical pseudo-problem in a particular way: it is the sort of problem that in its statement commits the fallacy of a complex question. This type of fallacy is committed when, in stating the question or problem, one tacitly takes for granted controversial assumptions that are not shared by all sides of the debate, or assumptions that are simply not true, or that indeed presuppose a false dichotomy. The result of engaging with a question so posed is that answers/solutions are either false or severely restricted by those same tacit assumptions implied by the question.

When evaluating a given ontology and the categories it introduces, philosophers tend to consider ontological and ideological economy. I discuss Quine's famous distinction between ontology (the entities that a theory claims exist) and ideology (the concepts and predicates that theoretical explanations rely upon) and the challenges one faces when attempting to measure them against one another. I also discuss the important distinction between simple and more complex ontological entities, and the widely held but questionable assumption that fundamentality and simplicity ought to go hand in hand in a metaphysical explanation.

I then move on to the meta-ontological discussion of the relationship between ontological entities, categories, and ontological roles. Following Oliver (1996), I suggest that the term "ontological category" should be reserved to pick out a particular ontological role that a philosopher finds in need of being filled in their theory, as they address a particular philosophical problem. Ontological entities, on the other hand, can fill one or multiple such roles, and thus can fall under one or more distinct ontological categories. This, I argue, tracks nicely what metaphysicians already tend to do – that is, it tracks how they assign distinct roles to distinct entities in their system and how they then employ such entities in different places in their overall metaphysical system. Of course, not everyone approaches ontological categories in this way; I conclude the section by contrasting this kind of bottom-up approach to ontological categories with descriptive and prescriptive top-down approaches.

Finally, in Section 4, I look at ways in which philosophers might break with some traditional category divisions and explore new ones. The search for the "correct" ontological categories, and the redrawing of different categorical divisions, carries a certain weight only if one assumes some form of realism about ontological categories. This is why I start the section by examining the circumscribed way that the discussion between an ontological realist and an ontological anti-realist about categories frequently plays out, and I find specific aspects of the dialectical exchange wanting. The anti-realist attacks tend to trivialize and misrepresent the endeavor that ontological realists are engaged in, while the realists often end up alienating more scientifically minded philosophers with their insistence that they are describing ultimate, immutable, and metaphysically necessary features of reality. I suggest in place of such a form of ontological realism, a more modest, cautious, revisionary form which might accommodate some of the anti-realist's complaints, without, however, giving up on the realist's overarching goals. I discuss the importance of trying to become aware of our metaphysical "blind spots" and the value of exploring new, nontraditional ontological categories and category systems. I argue that part of what constitutes progress in ontological inquiry has to do with opening ourselves up to different ways of conceiving of the familiar. Exploring new ontological entities and systems of categories is integral to that goal. To this end, I consider the example of Whitehead's original temporal ontology of events and objects, and the more recent approaches to gender categories as discussed by Barnes (2019).

From the description given so far, the reader will see that the approach of this Element is primarily methodological – it is a sort of "how to" guide to introducing ontological categories. My goal has not been to propose a single preferred system of ontological categories; such a project requires a more wide-ranging and in-depth discussion of a number of metaphysical problems, as well as a comparative analysis of different ontological systems. My goal has also not been to systematically describe the most commonly invoked ontological categories in metaphysical discussions, though a number of such categories do make an appearance. And my goal has certainly not been to engage in a meta-ontological study of the various ways that philosophers have employed, or ought to have employed, the concept of an "ontological category."

Instead, I have tried to illustrate, in some detail, by reference to the case study of universals, a number of concerns that are pertinent to metaphysical theory-building as one makes a case for a particular system of ontological categories. I have deliberately chosen to move between examining an ontological discussion at base level, and then looking at the parameters of the debate on a meta-level, because I think it is instructive. I firmly believe that taking the time to pay close attention to the main parameters of any given debate is crucial; and I find this is to be particularly important (though quite challenging) in fundamental ontology. By revealing and examining the underlying assumptions and parameters that are often taken for granted we start to become aware of the possibilities we weren't necessarily aware of before. There is also a value in providing illustrative examples from ground-level debates when discussing meta-theoretical issues. Too often in ontological discussions, we trail off into abstract discussion in which examples are hard to come by and the theoretical claims become esoteric and increasingly difficult to illustrate. Taking the time to explain, motivate, and provide examples is one way that we can keep our debates healthy and our metaphysical discussions intellectually honest. I have tried to do this here, but I assume that I too have failed in some places.

Of course, this methodological exploration of ontological categories is itself not neutral; it is carried out from a particular point of view, which makes it an opinionated one. I firmly believe that ontology is central to philosophy; that ontological categories are not merely features of our conceptual framework; and that universals are a genuine ontological category. I am thus a realist in more than one sense.

1 A Brief Historical Sketch

A historically informed approach to contemporary ontological debates is important for several reasons: it helps us understand better at the outset the historical context in which certain arguments and theories were developed and the assumptions that such a historical context might have left unexamined; it helps us understand those arguments in a contemporary setting, with new improvements, distinctions, and clarifications; in many circumstances, it helps us to build on the achievements of our predecessors rather than having to reinvent the wheel; and finally, one would hope, it helps guard us against repeating the mistakes of the past. In this section, due to space constraints, I can only provide a rough, bird's-eye view of the traditional realist approach to ontological categories and the types of skepticism that it gave rise to. It is noteworthy that any proposed list of categories immediately faces questions about method (the way that such a list is arrived at) and accuracy (whether it adequately captures the true divisions in the world).

1.1 Naïve Realism about Ontological Categories

It seems fair to say that the "traditional approach" to ontological categories originated with Plato and Aristotle, and that it carried a decidedly realist stamp. That is, these philosophers thought of fundamental categories of being as real mind-independent entities. Ancient philosophers were inclined to rely on natural language as a reliable guide to what there is. According to this view, there is a straightforward matchup between sentences such as "Xanthippe is wise" and what such sentences are about, namely, the particular woman – Xanthippe – and the property of *wisdom* she happens to have. The assumption of a straightforward matchup between our linguistic descriptions of reality and the ontological structure of reality is crucial for this outlook. Plato believed that an understanding of the world around us involves providing *definitions* of the true nature of things, and that this requires us to place those things in the correct *categories*, that is, under the correct Forms. Getting this right is essential, for it is the only way to find the real divisions in nature, it is the only way that one can, as Plato famously put it, “carve nature at its joints.”

Aristotle shared this general outlook with Plato, though he disagreed with the Platonic understanding of universals as independently existing Forms. Universals, for Aristotle, were *not* to be conceived in a Platonic way, as existing independently from particulars in a realm of their own; rather, he thought of the two types of entities as mutually dependent on one another. Aristotle’s grouping of entities also involves a much more diverse lot than just particulars and Forms; he lists the following ten as categories: substance, quantity, quality, relation, place, date, posture, state, action, and passion. This list was meant to be exhaustive and of the highest level of generality – for Aristotle, there was no further higher category that all of these categories could be subsumed under. But regardless of whether or not we find Aristotelian categories compelling today, what is important to recognize is that both Aristotle and Plato assumed a certain naïve form of realism about the categories: that is, they assumed that our categorizations of entities picked out genuine features of the outside world.

We can immediately see one difficulty that naïve realist assumptions give rise to: even a surface level comparison between Plato’s and Aristotle’s categorizations makes clear the discrepancy between what are arguably the most fundamental mind-independent features of reality. The two-category ontology of particulars and Forms is clearly quite different from the ten-category ontology described by Aristotle. What are we to make of such clashes between the category systems within the realist framework? One possibility is to argue that one philosopher’s category system is the correct one, while the other philosopher is simply wrong. Another possibility is to try reconciling the two systems of categories by showing that the more numerous category system is just an elaboration on the two-category one, and that it might be subsumed under it, with some modifications. A further possibility still is to claim that they are both wrong and that some other category system is the correct one. But the central problem underlying the disagreement is one concerning whether they have even employed the same *method* in arriving at their categorizations.

Indeed, how does one even go about deciding which categories there are? Interestingly, there has been significant controversy about what guided Aristotle in making the particular categorizations that he did, since he did not reveal his reasoning. Studtmann (2021) highlights four dominant interpretative approaches to Aristotelian categories – the question approach; the grammatical approach; the modal approach; and the medieval derivational approach. I want to draw attention only to the first two, since they seem to me to be the most likely interpretations and the most relevant to this discussion. The grammatical approach, as advocated by Baumer (1993), focuses on Aristotle's reliance on natural language and its inherent grammatical structure as a guide to categorizing entities in the world. The question approach, on the other hand, is promoted by Ackrill (1963) and it focuses on the questions one might ask about an entity. Take, for instance, a clever nine-year-old named Lulu; one can ask many questions about her: "What is Lulu?" could be answered with "Lulu is a nine-year-old human." Then one might ask, "What is a nine-year-old human?," to which one might answer, "it is an animal with particular sorts of features." Further questioning could then lead us to higher and higher categorizations, and ultimately to substance, as it was understood within Aristotle's framework. If we ask such questions about different sorts of beings in the world, we will, according to Ackrill, get the ten Aristotelian most general categories. The alternative line of questioning described by Ackrill does not press on with the same "What is X?" sort of question; rather it asks different specificatory questions about the X. So, for example, these questions could take the following shape: "What is Lulu?," "Where is Lulu?," "How old is Lulu?," "What is Lulu doing?," "How tall is Lulu?," and so on, until – again – presumably one arrives at the ten most fundamental Aristotelian categories.

I am not interested here in whether or not either of these approaches actually leads neatly to the Aristotelian list of categories. I merely want to point out that though at first glance it might seem correct to say that a philosopher might arrive at a list of categories by asking a number of questions about various entities, such a method is too haphazard. Take a nine-year-old from the example just given and imagine her performing a sorting exercise in a room surrounded by a variety of objects. How might she sort things? She might decide to sort them by color, shape, function, or she might decide to sort them by material that they are made out of, or she might sort them by whether or not they make a sound, or she might sort them by how pretty she finds them, or whether she finds them interesting or not, and so on and so forth. Clearly, there are a great many different ways that humans can sort things into groups and there are a great many different questions one can ask about any given thing and any given assortment of things. The search for ontological categories cannot be guided by such an unconstrained process of inquiry.

Thus, it should be clear that not just *any* type of question regarding entities will be conducive to finding *the most fundamental categories* of being. Even if one were to replace a child in the example discussed with Aristotle himself, the category system that the latter came up with would not be a better one just because it is devised by a famous philosopher rather than a child.[1] Rather, what

[1] A quick application of a version of the Euthyphro dilemma demonstrates this. If we ask, "What makes Aristotle's system of categories the correct one?," it would not be good to answer, "It is the correct one because it is chosen by Aristotle." Hopefully, it is a better system of categories

will make one system of categories better than another will have to do, at least in part, with the *types of questions* being asked about the structural features of the world. The questions need to be well-defined and the problems that they raise need to be well-articulated and motivated. It is only when metaphysicians postulate entities with specified explanatory roles that it becomes possible to compare the different types of entities and categories that philosophers employ in their different explanations. Without a certain amount of agreement on the philosophical problems that need to be addressed, and the type of methodology for solving such problems that should be employed, fundamental ontology risks looking like a solitary and idle endeavor, just one person's way of sorting things against another.

1.2 Three Forms of Skepticism about Categories

From the previous subsection, we can see that it is no surprise that a naïve realist approach to categories has historically suffered attacks from different directions. We can roughly distinguish three: (i) skepticism about whether the categories being described are indeed part of the structure of the world or are merely part of our conceptual framework with which we approach it; (ii) concern that the categorizations being taken for granted are wrong (perhaps it is not two types of entities that we should admit, but only one, or three, or four, or more); and (iii) questioning of our reliance on natural language as a guide to what there is, and efforts to provide better logical analyses of language as a way of getting to the correct ontological structure of reality.

Skepticism of the first kind goes back to Kant's *Critique of Pure Reason*, and it has had significant philosophical repercussions: on the one hand, we see that the worry that there is no way of arriving at genuine mind-independent categories has led philosophers to set their goals to more modestly defined descriptivist approaches to metaphysical categories, where the aim is to describe the concepts *we use* to understand the world, not the categories of the mind-independent world itself. Husserl's phenomenology and Strawson's descriptivist approach to metaphysics are two notable examples of this sort of attitude. On the other hand, the same Kantian worry has led some philosophers toward an idealism which takes the external world to be unknowable and the categories used to describe such a world as completely misleading and even contradictory. In this camp, we find British idealists such as F. H. Bradley developing vicious regress arguments against the possibility of external relations in an attempt to show that ontological pluralism is false and that ontological monism – a commitment to the existence of

because it describes the structure of reality more accurately, where the accuracy conditions are specified independently.

only one Absolute whole – must be the only true view of reality. Here too, we find McTaggart's notorious dismissal of the mind-independent existence of temporal series, based on his quick reductio arguments against the A-series and the B-series of time. Also going along with the idealist worldview we find Joachim's defense of the coherentist theory of truth with its obscure and mystifying reference to the indivisible Truth that only applies to the Absolute whole.

Skepticism of the second type mentioned – the one that is aimed at the number and types of categories introduced – is present in ancient Greek philosophy, and is even more visible in the Middle Ages with respect to the ancients' particular–universal distinction. For instance, Aquinas, Duns Scotus, Ockham, and others are often seen as early supporters of the one-category trope ontology. Building on disagreements concerning the type and the number of categories introduced, one can quickly arrive at skepticism concerning the method – whether there can be a right way at arriving at the fundamental categories at all.

One can then see how the two types of skepticism just described influenced the third type, which takes aim at *natural language* as a guide to ontological categories. We see this very clearly in early Russell, with his break from idealists and commitment to the careful logical analysis of language as a guide to the correct logical structure of the world. Note that this third type of skepticism is quite limited – it does not renounce the project of discovering the correct ontological categories altogether. Rather, it merely corrects the route; it requires that the project be carried out through careful logical analysis. Early Wittgenstein in *Tractatus*, at least in parts, seemed to be on this track too. In other parts, of course, he famously denounced the very possibility of metaphysics and our ability to make any sense of it.

Subsequently, the logical positivists' insistence on naturalism and a posteriori method of inquiry led to an even stronger anti-metaphysical and anti-ontological sentiment that dominated the decades that followed. Insistence on a posteriori inquiry and continuity with science seemingly left no room for questions about ontological categories. Whatever was left of the "old philosophy" got translated into merely linguistic approaches to what were once considered substantive philosophical problems.

But despite the logical positivists' best efforts to leave metaphysics behind, a number of them were not able to practice what they preached, and they found themselves unable to resist ontological discussions. This irony was not lost on Gustav Bergmann, who joined the Vienna Circle in the late 1920s and early 1930s, but found himself increasingly disagreeing with some of the main tenets of the Circle. Indeed, by the early 1950s, Bergmann's philosophy had already taken an "ontological turn." He thought that metaphysics was, in fact, unavoidable and that many of the logical positivists were tacitly committing themselves to various ontological and metaphysical theses. He made this critique clear in his suggestively titled collection of papers *The Metaphysics of Logical Positivism* (1953). In the years that followed, Bergmann revived many of the traditional ontological questions, including questions about the types of ontological entities that should be admitted and how those entities relate to one another. His own approach to these questions was heavily influenced by a post-Russellian search for an "ideal language" whose ontological commitments would be transparent. But perhaps most importantly for our purposes, Bergmann marks a forceful return to realism about ontological categories. He was the first to use the phrase "ontological ground" and to use it ubiquitously in making arguments for why one might need to admit a certain category of entity.

Quine's criticism of the logical empiricists' analytic–synthetic distinction refocused attention on ontology. With the breaking down of the boundary between the two domains, Quine hoped to show that philosophical inquiry was continuous with science and could, in fact, be carried out with the same scientific rigor and in a naturalistic spirit. To help make metaphysical discussion more regimented, Quine tried to impose certain meta-ontological constraints. He proposed an explicit criterion of ontological commitment ("to be is to be a value of a bound variable" in statements of first-order logic); he urged metaphysicians to provide clear identity criteria for entities they wanted to postulate ("no entity without identity"); and he offered a cost–benefit approach to evaluating opposing metaphysical theories (by appeal to a trade-off between ideology and ontology, and appeals to simplicity and explanatory power). This had a double effect: on the one hand, it freed up ontology in a way that allowed many different theories with different ontological commitments to flourish and compete with one another; on the other hand, the proliferation of different ontologies, together with Quine's impactful instrumentalist approach to philosophical theories, gave momentum to ontological relativism.

This brief and inevitably broad-strokes sketch of the way that the fundamental ontological question concerning categories has been approached is a project that deserves further attention and careful historical development in its own right. My goal here is not to take on such a project in any real depth, but just to highlight some ideas that shaped the debate about the very possibility of the ontological project. It helps to know, for instance, that the heavily naturalist approaches exemplified by many metaphysicians today, as well as the popularity of different nominalist approaches to ontology, can be traced back to Quine and his taste "for desert landscapes." Similarly, it's good to keep in mind that the scientific realist approach to ontology has its roots in Bergmann and his students' reckoning with logical positivism, on the one hand, as well as in John Anderson's influence on David Armstrong and the Australian school of metaphysics, on the other.

It is thanks to figures like David Armstrong, David Lewis, Keith Campbell, D. C. Williams, E. J. Lowe, and others who engaged in substantial ontological debates during the last few decades of the twentieth century, that ontology is a much livelier field today than it was 100 years ago.

This ontological revival is in no small measure due to what might be termed "the truthmaker turn" in metaphysics, advocated for by Armstrong and C. B. Martin. The truthmaker principle that they advocated marked a strong return to the correspondence theory of truth and its main idea that the truth of a sentence consists in its correspondence to reality. The truthmaker principle thus requires that all truths need to be made true by something in reality – a *truth-maker*. The principle itself does not legislate as to which truthmakers need to be admitted in order to make various truthbearers true, nor does it require a simple one-to-one correspondence between true sentences and truthmakers. (The same truthmaker can make multiple sentences true and one truth can have multiple truthmakers.) Nor does the truthmaker principle require us to naïvely read ontology off the surface structure of a sentence. But what the truthmaker-led debate has done is to refocus attention back on ontological entities and categories that need to be admitted to anchor the truths of our statements about the world.

2 Introducing an Ontological Category: A Case Study in Universals

This section tells a story of how universals – one of the oldest, most disputed, but also most worked-out ontological categories – got introduced. Universals are particularly relevant to our discussion because right from their inception, they were thought of as filling a dual role: they were thought of as an *ontological category* as well as an entity that helped *categorize* other entities. I discuss the "one-over-many" argument for universals as it was presented by Plato, as well as the way that the argument was developed by a prominent contemporary realist about universals – David Armstrong. Armstrong believed that his version of "one over many" only offered a "preliminary case" for universals, not a decisive one. His case for universals includes the argument from laws of nature and the so-called negative arguments, from Russell, against the denial of relational universals; and from Pap and Jackson, from the lack of adequate paraphrases of apparent references to universals.

2.1 The Original One-over-Many Argument for Universals

Plato introduced universals in the context of searching for an adequate Socratic definition. His dialogues frequently open with Socrates asking a question of the type, "What is *X*?" about relevant ethical or aesthetic qualities such as virtue, justice, beauty, and so on. The right answer to this kind of question, according to Plato, had to take the form of a *definition* of *X*. And yet not just any definition would do. The definition that Plato was after was not supposed to merely list the sort of things that were considered to be *X*; nor would it have been sufficient to explain just the meaning of the *word* "*X*." What Plato wanted the correct Socratic definition to do was to explain the very *nature of the quality X*: it had to give a universally true description of its essence. It had to be a definition that would guide us in deciding whether various new candidates were indeed *X* or not.

Thus, right at the outset, Plato was making an ontological distinction between many things that exemplify *X*, on the one hand, and the single entity *X* itself, on the other. He contrasts the plurality of just actions with *justice* itself, the plurality of beautiful things with *beauty* itself, and so on. In the same breath, though, Plato stresses that what makes various things beautiful and just is their partaking in the "absolute" beauty and justice:

> It seems to me that whatever else is beautiful apart from absolute beauty is beautiful because it partakes of that absolute beauty, and for no other reason. . . . The one thing that makes that object beautiful is the presence in it or association with it, in whatever way the relation comes about, of absolute beauty. I do not go so far as to insist upon the precise details – only upon the fact that it is by beauty that beautiful things are beautiful. (*Phaedo* 100 c–d, Plato 1963, pp. 81–82)

Beauty itself, *justice* itself, the *X* itself are entities Plato called Forms and in the passage quoted we already see at work the famous "one-over-many" argument for the existence of Forms.[2] The argument proceeds from the assumption that many different particular things – say, *a*, *b*, and *c* – are all beautiful, to the conclusion that there must be a single Form of beauty that is responsible for conferring beauty to the particular things. This movement, from the plurality of things that have something in common to a conclusion that asserts the existence of the entity that the plurality of entities shares in, is even more explicit in the following passage from the *Republic* 596a–b:

> We are in the habit, I take it, of positing a single idea or form in the case of the various multiplicities to which we give the same name. . . . Let us take any multiplicity you please; for example, there are many couches and tables. . . . But these utensils imply, I suppose, only two ideas or forms, one of a couch and one of a table. (Plato 1963, p. 820)

[2] The name of the argument comes from Aristotle who referred to an argument that Platonists used for the existence of Forms. Plato himself never actually used the phrase but he did sometimes refer to a Form as being the "one over many."

We can see here that the distinction between Forms and particulars that partake in those Forms marks for Plato a difference between *two different ontological categories* that occupy two separate realms of being, and that have contrasting features. Forms are the more perfect, single, independent, changeless entities, whereas particulars are less perfect, multiple entities that have their natures in virtue of their relations to Forms, and they are subject to constant change.

Why Plato held that Forms exist independently of particulars is not entirely clear. His arguments for this seem to be based on the assumption that there are perfect properties that particular things never fully exemplify, but only approximate to. Mathematics, and geometry in particular, provided Plato with plenty of examples of this sort: for instance, one can speak of a perfectly circular shape but whichever circle we draw it's always going to have some irregularity and imperfection. This led Plato to believe that things in the natural world can only approximate the perfection described by a mathematician. Generalizing to all particulars, he thought that they could only approximate to the perfection of Forms; that is, even though perfect justice may never be encountered in any just action that any one person performs, perfect justice, that is, the Form of *justice*, must exist, as a perfect paradigm.

Plato described the relation between the particulars and Forms in two different ways: sometimes he described it as *participation* or *sharing in*, and sometimes as *imitation*. In the first case, particulars *participate in* the Form or the Form is somehow shared by particulars; the second case is more mysterious: particulars are related to the Forms as imperfect copies are to the originals. Since Forms possess the ultimate perfection and particulars are only poor copies of it, Forms were thought of by Plato as having greater reality.

In *Parmenides*, Plato addressed the issue of how inclusive his realm of Forms should be. Moral and aesthetic qualities such as *justice*, *beauty*, and *goodness* seem to deserve honorary membership in the realm, but what about Forms of *man*, *fire*, or *water*? In *Parmenides*, the young Socrates discloses his puzzlement and inability to decide such cases as well as a reluctance to admit less dignified Forms of things like hair, or mud, or dirt, and so on. Parmenides' response to this is that when he gets older he will learn not to be so fastidious and discriminatory when it comes to Forms.

Plato's discussion of "lesser" Forms is analogous to the distinction that contemporary metaphysicians make between sparse properties and relations, the sharing of which makes for genuine resemblance between particulars, and abundant properties and relations the sharing of which does not make for resemblance. A contemporary realist about universals tends to draw this distinction by saying that the former properties correspond to universals while the latter don't; similarly, Plato allowed some properties to be Forms and not others.

Although it might seem that Plato's Socrates is basing his decisions on ad hoc judgments about which properties and relations *appear* worthy of a place in the realm of Forms, the grounds for the distinction run deeper. This can be especially appreciated in Plato's later writings, in which his earlier conception of Forms as paradigms gives way to the conception of Forms as *categorizers*. Therein, Plato makes it very clear that not just any collection of particulars corresponds to a Form; only the collections that respect the "objective articulations" in nature are eligible. This view is confirmed by the following passages from the *Statesman* 262b–e, where Plato cannot stress enough the importance of following the true classifications of things in pursuit of the correct Socratic definition:

> We must only divide where there is a real cleavage between specific forms. The section must always possess a specific form. . . . [I]t is dangerous, Socrates, to chop reality up into small portions. It is always safer to go down the middle to make our cuts. The real cleavages among the Forms are more likely to be found thus, and the whole art of these definitions consists in finding these cleavages. (Plato 1963, pp. 1025–1026)

"Real cleavages" in the world are cleavages between the classes of genuinely resembling particulars. To each of those classes corresponds a Form which unites it. To avoid mistakes of misclassification one has to be careful and try not to give in to hasty and arbitrary divisions dictated by one's own subjective interests. The example of such a mistake is:

> The kind of mistake a man would make who, seeking to divide the class of human beings in two, divided them into Greeks and barbarians. This is a division most people in this part of the world make. They separate the Greeks from all other nations making them a class apart; thus they group all other nations together as a class, ignoring the fact that it is an indeterminate class made up of peoples who have no intercourse with each other and speak different languages. Lumping all this non-Greek residue together, *they think it must constitute one real class because they have a common name "barbarian" to attach to it*. . . . A division setting Lydians or Phrygians or any other peoples in contradistinction to all the rest can only be made when a man fails to arrive at a *true division into two groups each of which after separation is not only a portion of the whole class to be divided but also a real subdivision of it*. (Plato 1963, p. 1026, italics mine)

This passage is an important one, as it clearly illustrates how concerned Plato was about making "real" classifications as opposed to hasty and confused groupings that only on the surface *appear* to belong together. The key to correct classifications is finding *genuine* resemblances between the members of a given class – where there is such resemblance, there is a corresponding Form; where there isn't, there is no corresponding Form. Thus Forms turn out to be not just one of the most fundamental ontological categories introduced, alongside particulars, but are themselves are entities that sort and categorize.

This dual role that Forms are meant to play leads to a problem that is brought out by Plato's infamous *Third Man Argument*, an infinite regress argument which exhibits the following structure:

(1) *a*, *b*, and *c* are all large because there is a Form of largeness *L* that they all participate in.
(2) *a*, *b*, *c*, and *L* are all large because there is a Form of largeness L_1 that they all participate in.
(3) *a*, *b*, *c*, *L*, and L_1 are all large because all of them participate in a Form of largeness L_2 – and so on ad infinitum.

Three main assumptions are at work in this argument. First is "one over many" which states that many things being *L* must be explained by the existence of the Form *L* that all of them participate in. The second premise is implicit and it has been called the premise of "non-self explanation"; it simply assumes, that in explaining what *a*, *b*, *c*, and *L* have in common one cannot appeal to the *L* itself, but needs to appeal to a *different* Form of largeness, L_1. The third premise which is implied in this argument is the "self-partaking" premise; it assumes that the Form *L* is itself *L*, or, in this particular case, that the Form of largeness is itself large.

The correct interpretation of this argument has been debated at length by commentators on Plato. My aim here is not to engage in detail with that debate, but to merely point out the tension that it brings out very clearly – namely, Forms conceived as entities that confer to particulars their nature (in this instance *largeness* to *a*, *b*, and *c*), then need some other Form to confer that nature to them (since largeness is itself assumed to be large). But if there is a different, higher-order Form of largeness that confers largeness L_1 to *L*, then we are off on a regress of higher and higher-order Forms.

It might seem that the easiest way to escape this difficulty would be to claim that Forms have a dual role: the role of conferring qualities to particulars *as well as* the role of conferring that very same quality to itself – the form of *largeness* would itself be large due to this self-conferring feature. But the outcome of this approach is a very real puzzle about what it means for a Form itself to be large or beautiful or just, and so on (since these appear to be qualities that particular things have, not Forms themselves). To avoid this puzzle, Plato would have to embrace the alternative and claim that Forms confer qualities to particulars but do not themselves exemplify such qualities – so the Form of largeness is not itself large and the Form of beauty is not itself beautiful, and so on. This would nicely avoid the Third Man regress altogether, leaving Plato with the task of explaining of how the Forms confer beauty, justice, virtue, and so on to particulars, if they are themselves distinctly *not* those things.

Although Aristotle disagreed with Plato on the nature of Forms and their interaction with particulars, he did believe in the existence of some such entities. He called them *ta katholou,* that is, universals. The main point of disagreement was over Plato's view of Forms as entities completely independent of, and separately existing from, particulars. Plato saw Forms as entities in a realm of their own, outside of space and time, and yet more real than particulars. Aristotle, on the other hand, wanted to restore the balance in favor of particulars. Particulars and universals are seen as mutually dependent entities; in fact, it is an essential part of the nature of Aristotelian universals to be related to particulars. The reason why Plato could not see this, according to Aristotle, was because he understood Forms to be *substances*. In his earlier works, such as *Categories*, Aristotle uses the term "substance" to refer to things that are neither *in* anything nor *said of* anything; they are things like a particular horse or a particular man. Thus, Plato's mistake, in Aristotle's view, was that his Forms were more like particular substances than universals.

Although he harshly criticized the outcome of the argument – the existence of *Forms* as such – Aristotle fully appropriated and relied upon the "one-over-many" argument as proof of the existence of his own universals. Indeed, he took the validity of the ontological version of the argument for granted and employed different versions of "one over many" for different purposes. For instance, Aristotle mentions a version of the argument when arguing for the existence of universals as objects/contents of thought and knowledge. In *Posterior Analytics*, he describes the inductive process that leads from the perception and memory of numerous objects to the universal "that is one apart from the many" and "one and the same in all those things" as a "principle skill of understanding" (100a4–9). In *Metaphysics*, he states that "if there is nothing apart from individuals, there will be no object of thought" and as a consequence of this, "all things will be objects of sense" (999b1–2). Thus, for Aristotle, if there are no universals there is nothing that we can properly think about; and without thought there is no knowledge, "for the knowledge of anything is universal" (1003a14).

To summarize, Plato relied upon the "one-over-many" argument to provide him with the entities he needed for definitions of the natures of things – to explain what made different things beautiful, just, wise, large, and so on. These entities were Forms, the self-sufficient, independent, immutable, perfect, and eternal entities existing in a realm of their own. In his earlier writings, Plato thought of Forms as perfect paradigms, but later came to think of them as entities that categorize other entities and through such categorizations reflect the objective, mind-independent classifications of reality. The exact way that Forms were meant to fulfill this role remains unclear.

The way that Plato went about introducing universals left a lot of his assumptions implicit. For instance, he took it for granted that the phenomenon that he was describing (different particulars seemingly having a common nature) was an obvious and indisputable one. He also took it for granted that this phenomenon was inherently problematic and in need of an explanation. He then assumed that introducing an entity – a Form – would provide an adequate explanation of the phenomenon in question. Finally, Plato did not question the existence and the role that multiple distinct particulars play. The assumption was that the universals help explain the natures and the proper groupings of many different particulars, but that the particulars themselves were in no need of special argument or explanation. As we will see in the next section, more recent arguments for the existence of universals attempt to make some of these assumptions more explicit and motivated.

2.2 A Contemporary Approach to Universals: Armstrong's Use of the One-over-Many Argument

The contemporary realists' reliance on the "one-over-many" argument is more guarded than Plato's and Aristotle's, but the argument still presents the main motivating force for the introduction of universals as a sui generis ontological category. David Armstrong, one of the most prominent contemporary realists, puts it this way: "[t]he main argument for the existence of universals is Plato's 'One over Many'. I do not think that it proves straight off that there are universals. But I think that it shows that there is a strong preliminary case for accepting universals" (Armstrong 1997a, p. 101).

This "strong preliminary case" is built on the fundamental assumption that facts of sameness of type are objective "Moorean" facts:

> G.E. Moore thought . . . that there are many facts which even philosophers should not deny, whatever philosophical account or analysis they gave of these facts. He gave as an example the existence of his hands. We can argue about the philosophical account which ought to be given of material objects, such as Moore's hands. But we should not deny that there are such things. . . . I suggest that the fact of sameness of type is a Moorean fact. (Armstrong 1997a, p.102)

Calling the sameness of type a "Moorean fact" makes it very clear what Armstrong takes to be the starting point of the ontological debate. The apparent sameness of type is something that all sides of the debate should agree upon, according to him. The explanation of this fact, on the other hand, is the issue about which philosophers disagree. Armstrong himself believes that apparent sameness of type is due to genuine resemblance between particular things, and that this resemblance is due to partial identity. The structure of Armstrong's version of the "one-over-many" argument is thus roughly as follows:

(1) Facts of sameness of type are Moorean facts, that is, objective facts that no philosopher should deny.
(2) Apparent sameness of type should be *explained.*
(3) Genuine resemblance among different particular things is what gives rise to the apparent sameness of type among distinct particulars.
(4) Genuine resemblance among different particulars is due to their having something in common, literally sharing something.
(5) Universals are what different resembling particulars have in common and what makes them resemble each other.

Plato's version of "one over many" took for granted (1), (2), and (3) and directly inferred (5) from (4).

Armstrong's structure of the argument, on the other hand, is more careful and allows opponents to disagree at various points. Contra Armstrong, one might try to deny (1). This denial could be developed in different ways. Theoretically, one might deny that there is even an appearance of sameness of type. This is a difficult claim to pull off, since it goes against what most people report as their experience of reality; thus, one would have to appeal to a very different phenomenological experience of reality – one which does not recognize similarities and patterns in nature at all. Communication with someone who makes such a claim would be impossible, since the very structure of our language and our thought relies on a shared understanding of commonalities and patterns; thus, even the denial of the appearance of such patterns would, in its formulation and communication, presuppose the very things which are being denied. A more plausible denial of (1) would acknowledge that there is indeed an appearance of sameness of type, but deny that such an appearance captures a *real* phenomenon. In reality, the claim would go, there is no genuine resemblance between particulars, no Moorean *fact* of sameness of type; there is only an apparent fact. The interesting question then becomes analogous to those that other skeptical attacks give rise to – namely, how come there is a need to postulate the sameness of type when in reality there isn't one? What gives rise to such a pervasive illusion and what, if anything, is to be found in its stead? An error theory of some sort is called for.

Armstrong was correct in his assessment that most philosophers would not outright deny (1), and would indeed agree that there are many objective resemblances to be found in reality. But such philosophers may disagree about (2); that is, they may disagree on whether an *explanation* of such facts is necessary at all. For instance, nominalists tend to reject outright the demand for an *analysis* of the facts of resemblance and insist on taking them to be primitive. In Quine's words: "That the houses and roses and sunsets are all of them red may be taken as ultimate and irreducible" (Quine 1997, p. 81) Along similar lines, David Lewis remarks:

> An effort at systematic philosophy must indeed give an account of any purported fact. There are three ways to give an account. (1) "I deny it" – this earns a failing mark if the fact is really Moorean. (2) "I analyse it thus" – this is Armstrong's response to the fact of apparent sameness of type. Or (3) "I accept it as primitive." Not every account is an *analysis*! A system that takes certain Moorean facts as primitive, as unanalysed, cannot be accused of failing to make a place for them. (Lewis 1983, p. 20)

This is a forceful response to Armstrong, and, alongside him, to any realist who insists on the need for an *explanation* of facts of resemblance. Lewis believes that "making a place" for a phenomenon in one's philosophical system ought to count as a good enough response. He writes:

> An adequate Nominalism . . . is a theory that takes Moorean facts of apparent sameness of type as primitive. It predicates mutual resemblance of the things which are apparently of the same type; or it predicates naturalness of some property that they all share, i.e. that has them all as members; and it declines to analyse these predications any further. (Lewis 1983, p. 21)

One can debate whether taking a phenomenon as primitive and unanalyzable amounts to a sufficient engagement, and I will have more to say about in Section 3.2.3. What is worth highlighting in this Armstrong–Lewis exchange is the value of an open debate concerning whether a certain phenomenon should receive further analysis at all, especially when such an analysis quickly leads to the introduction of a new ontological category. Indeed, if we embark on providing a reductive analysis of facts of resemblance, we are already halfway to introducing the category of universals. The subsequent steps, as we will see shortly, are to analyze resemblance in terms of partial identity, and then to admit universals as the entities that ground that partial identity between particulars.

2.2.1 Universals as Entities That Ground Resemblance

As Armstrong himself openly acknowledged, there is nothing in the "one-over-many" argument that *compels* us to draw the conclusion that universals exist. The ontological inflation that takes place is not necessitated by the argument. But very few things in metaphysics ever are. What we are offered is an *explanation* of resemblance in terms of universals.

The explanation runs as follows: genuine resemblances among different particulars are nothing else but identity in a certain respect. For example, two apples resembling in being red and round is due to their being strictly identical in those respects; the two apples have parts which are numerically identical in both and which make for their partial identity – these parts are the universal of *redness* and the universal of *roundness*. Universals are thus the sorts of entities that can multiply occur and that are identical in each of their occurrences; our intuition that things that resemble each other literally have the same thing in common is thus given an ontological ground.

With universals, a realist is able to explain a few other features of resemblance. Two things that share all their universals are exact duplicates – they could be said to *perfectly resemble* one another. Perfect resemblance understood as sharing all the respects of resemblance is transitive: if *a* perfectly resembles *b*, and *b* perfectly resembles *c*, then *a* will perfectly resemble *c* (since all three will be perfect duplicates). This is obviously not the case when resemblance is less than perfect, since the universals that *a* and *b* share may not all be the same universals that *b* and *c* share.

One can also account for degrees of resemblance among particulars in terms of universals: one way of doing this would be to say that particulars resemble to a larger degree if they share more universals, and to a lesser degree if they share fewer universals. But this is perhaps a somewhat crude criterion, as it is easy to imagine two particulars, *a* and *b*, sharing one universal *F*, say *being human*, but resembling each other more than *a* and *c*, which share two universals *G* and *H*, say *having black hair* and *having brown eyes* (where, for example, *a* and *b* are two children and *c* is an adult poodle). In this case we would be judging resemblances according to which universals "carry more weight" by capturing respects of resemblance better.

In any case, genuine, deep, resemblances between particulars are few. A scientific realist like Armstrong believes that which universals there are is indeed an a posteriori matter: it is up to scientific theories to discover the real cleavages in nature and thus provide the candidates for universals.[3] According to this sort of scientific realist, most of our everyday talk about the sharing of properties and relations is actually not a talk about *genuine* resemblances in nature.

2.2.2 Genuine Resemblances without Universals

Metaphysicians can agree with Armstrong's setup of the "one over many" and accept (1), (2), and (3) – that there is indeed a Moorean fact of the sameness of

[3] Of different scientific inquires, Armstrong favors physics, and believes that it will give us our ultimate, most fundamental universals.

type and that it is indeed due to genuine resemblance among different particulars – but refuse to analyze this fact any further, and thus refuse to postulate the category of universals. This is the move that nominalists such as David Lewis make when they deny the existence of universals and take resemblance as a primitive.[4]

Nominalism

More specifically, Lewis defines properties as sets of all of their instances: actual *and* possible. For him, *redness* is to be identified with the set of *all* red things – across actual and possible worlds. Thus, the only kind of entity admitted in Lewis's ontology are particulars and classes of particulars. The need to admit particulars in other possible worlds alongside this-worldly particulars was prompted by the coextension problem. If properties are nothing more than sets of their instances, then properties that have the same extensions (such as, say, the property of *having a heart* and the property of *having a kidney*) amount to being the same property. By appeal to *possibilia*, Lewis was able to address this difficulty: namely, although the set of people with hearts is ordinarily the same as the set of people with kidneys, this is considered to be merely a contingent feature of people in this world; when one considers possible worlds and their inhabitants, the two sets of instances come apart.

With the coextension problem addressed, Lewis still worried that his account of properties was too undiscriminating, that it did not capture real resemblance among its members. He wrote: Because properties are so abundant, they are undiscriminating. Any two things share infinitely many properties, and fail to share infinitely many others. That is so whether the two things are perfect duplicates or utterly dissimilar. Thus properties do nothing to capture facts of resemblance. That is work more suited to the sparse universals (Lewis 1983, p. 13).

Lewis then went on to introduce "an elite minority of special properties" – the natural properties –which were meant to capture genuine resemblance classes. These were envisioned, essentially, as a class nominalist's response to universals: "we could call a property *perfectly* natural if its members are all and only those things that share some one universal" (Lewis 1983, p. 13). But Lewis's ontology did not accept universals and his appeal to them here is merely illustrative. What he wanted was that his own ontological categories would

[4] I am here using the term "nominalism" to refer to views that reject universals and construe properties out of ordinary particulars. Trope theories are not nominalist in this sense, for they tend to construe particulars out of property-instances. If we were to adopt the view that any denial of universals is a nominalist view, then Lewis's view as well as all the varieties of trope theoretic views would count as nominalist. I am not using the terminology in this way, however, and am following Armstrong (1978, 1980, 1983, 1997) in my usage.

somehow be able to do the work that universals do in the realist's ontology. He grappled with this issue and considered two avenues: the first was to take "naturalness" as a primitive predicate (see Lewis 1983, p. 14) which applies to all and only natural classes (resemblance would then be explained as a relation holding among the members of natural classes picked out by such primitive predicates); the second was to take genuine resemblance as a primitive relation and then provide a definition of natural properties in its terms (as properties whose members are all and only the members that resemble each other). He did not adjudicate between these two paths and evaluating them further need not concern us here. What should be mentioned is that the same difficulties also assail the more recent version of nominalism –Rodriguez-Pereyra's (2002) brand of resemblance nominalism and its commitment to primitive predicates of resemblance.

Despite the above-mentioned difficulties, both the class nominalism of David Lewis and the resemblance nominalism of Rodriguez-Pereyra explicitly acknowledge that facts of resemblance are real mind-independent features of reality. This is not the case for predicate and concept nominalists who take resemblance between two particulars to consist in sharing the same predicate or falling under the same concept. A predicate nominalist claims that different particulars resemble each other in being red due to the fact that they *fall under* the predicate "is red," while the concept nominalist appeals to the concept of redness. But predicates and concepts are created by us, and it appears wrong-headed to claim that properties of things depend on the existence of the predicates we make to describe them or the concepts we create for them to fall under. To put it slightly differently: if there were no humankind, and thus no spoken language, there would still seemingly be things that were red, square, had mass or charge, and so on, and resembled other particulars in some of these respects. Moreover, it seems plausible to assume that there are already resemblances and properties in the actual world that we do not yet have predicates or concepts for. But a predicate or a concept nominalist would have to deny this – the properties would only come into existence once we have found predicates or concepts to describe them. Or, perhaps they would have to appeal to such things as *possible* predicates or concepts that await our discovery of them. Either way, this kind of nominalist story seems rather implausible.

Trope Theory

Trope theorists have argued for a midway position between the realist and the nominalist approach, introducing a sui generis entity – a nonrepeatable, singly occurring sort of property they call a "trope." Trope theorists such as

Keith Campbell tend to think of their theory as primarily particularist: "The trope theory is Particularist. It accepts Locke's thesis that all things are always only particular. It denies that there are any literally common elements present in all members of a group of resembling particulars" (Campbell 1990, p. 27).

But although it accepts only particulars in its ontology and denies any universals whatsoever, trope theory should not be confused with a nominalist position:

> Some writers use the label "nominalist" for every denial of universals, but this blurs a crucial distinction: ordinary nominalisms, in denying universals, deny the existence of *properties*, except perhaps as shadows of predicates or classifications. They recognize only concrete particulars and sets. . . . But the trope philosophy emphatically *affirms* the existence of properties (qualities and relations). Indeed, it holds that there is *nothing but* properties (or nothing but properties and space–time). However, it insists that these properties are not universals but, on the contrary, particulars with a single, circumscribed occurrence. (Campbell 1990, p. 27)

In this paragraph, Campbell changes the terms of discussion – the division is no longer between realists who believe in the existence of universals and nominalists who deny it. Properties have now become central and, since nominalists construe properties out of particulars (plus sets, resemblance relations, etc.), their properties appear to Campbell not to have enough ontological weight; he says they are mere "shadows of predicates or classifications." The trope theorist, on the other hand, "emphatically *affirms*" the existence of properties, which for them means that there are ontological entities filling this particular property role. In fact, for Campbell, "there is *nothing but* properties."

When it comes to the problem of sameness of type, Campbell is very much in agreement with Armstrong that the problem is a serious one that a "responsible ontology" ought to tackle: "The world is not a chaos, with every aspect, at every minute, unique in character. Nor is it an undifferentiated blancmange. It is a diverse and orderly cosmos displaying patterns of recurrence. No responsible ontology can evade this very general fact; and no responsible ontology can avoid offering its assay of this situation" (Campbell 1990, p. 28).

Thus, just like the realist and the class and resemblance nominalists mentioned, the trope theorist also recognizes the importance of the Moorean facts of resemblance. Campbell clearly agrees with (1), (2), and (3) in Armstrong's version of the "one over many" outlined in Section 2.2. Unlike Lewis, and more along the realist's lines, Campbell recognizes the importance of providing an "assay of this situation." At the same time, Campbell believes that the realist's stating of the problem should be broken down into two related but separate questions – the questions he refers to as "*A*" and "*B*." The "*A* question" is about the single particular object and its properties; it is a question that takes "*one* single red object" and asks of it, "what is it about this thing in virtue of which it is red?" The "*B* question," on the other hand, is about two or more objects; it is a question that takes "any *two* red things" and asks, "what is it about these two things in virtue of which they are both red?"

Campbell points out that discussions of the problem of universals mostly assume that the two questions are to be given parallel answers. This can be seen from the fact that the realist gives the same response to *A* and *B* – that the single thing is red in virtue of the universal redness present in it, and that two things are both red in virtue of the universal of redness present in each. The conclusion that Campbell draws from this is that: "The conflation of the *A* and the *B* questions is responsible for making the realist position seem much more inevitable than it really is" (Campbell 1990, p. 29). By disentangling the two questions he hopes to show that the realist's solution is not inevitable.

For Campbell, once the two questions are separated, universals start to seem somewhat ad hoc as an answer to the *A* question. In his view, it amounts to saying, without any further justification, that "a nature or a character of an item can never be particular." Or, if one is in search of a more "scientific" answer to the question of what it is in virtue of which some object has a certain property, the quest is delayed a little. The property in question will be explained away by some other property (or properties) of the underlying structure and those by, perhaps, other properties. However, Campbell insists, there will be a moment in which the only available answer to a question such as "what is it *about charge* in virtue of which it is charge?" would be "its being what it is" (Campbell 1990, p. 30). This sort of tautological response is inevitable at a certain level of every system:

> It is critical to the trope vision of the world that particulars can be natures, that something can just *be* a case of charge, or colour, or whatever. Philosophers are rightly suspicious of tautological-seeming answers to questions . . . but it is important to remember that such answers arise at some point in *every* system. The realist about universals has a substantial seeming answer to our A question, even in the case of basic properties. But the rock bottom is not far away. What is it about electric charge in virtue of which the presence of this universal is necessary and sufficient for something's having charge? Its being what it is. (Campbell 1990, p. 30)

In other words, something's having electric charge may come down to its having the right sort of universal, but the next question about that universal – "what is it about that universal that enables the particular to have electric charge?" – would then have no informative answer; it would probably have to be something like "it being that particular type of universal." The point of these observations, for Campbell, is to show that introducing universals in order to give a slightly more substantial answer to the *A* question is an ontological redundancy, unless, of course, universals are required elsewhere in one's ontology.

Campbell might be right about the fact that an answer to an *A* question alone is not a good enough reason for introducing universals. But the realist's main argument for the existence of universals comes from trying to answer the *B* question – in virtue of what do two or more objects resemble each other in being red, round, human, and so on? It is the intuition about there being certain *shared natures* among different particulars that motivates the introduction of universals. With universals, realists take themselves to have provided an *explanatory* answer to the *B* question, along with a "more substantial answer" to the *A* question.

In contrast, Campbell's own answer to the *B* question is that the apparent sameness of type is simply due to the presence in them of distinct resembling tropes:

> What is it about two objects in virtue of which they are both red? Each includes a red trope. What is it about those tropes in virtue of which they are both red tropes? Their likeness to one another is what makes them tropes of the same kind. Their natures make this the red, rather than the blue, or oblong, kind. . . . What is being offered here, of course, is a Resemblance theory of resemblance and recurrence, an assay in terms of resembling particulars, in place of one involving identical universals. It takes resemblance to be ultimately, in basic cases, unanalysable. (Campbell 1990, p. 31)

Thus, resemblance of tropes themselves, just as in the case of class and resemblance nominalism, is to remain a given and not a further analyzable feature of trope theory.[5]

2.3 Additional Arguments for Universals

I have thus far presented "one over many" as the realist's "strong preliminary case" for universals. But realists tend to support their case with additional arguments. For instance, Armstrong also wants his theory of universals to sustain his non-Humean account of laws of nature. According to this account, roughly, "All *F*s are *G*s" is a law of nature only if there is a second-order law-making relation of necessitation, *N*, holding between the universals' *F*-ness

[5] For a more thorough discussion of trope theory, good starting points are Simons (1994) and Maurin (2018).

and *G*-ness: *N* (*F*, *G*). Armstrong (1983, 1997b) singles out functional laws as laws that have the best claim to be fundamental, and determinable universals as the ones that ought to feature in them. One example of a functional law is Newton's law of gravitation: it correlates the determinables *force*, *mass*, and *distance*, and under each of these determinables there is a class with possibly an infinite many determinate universals that the law applies to.

Additionally, there have also been some prominent "negative arguments" for universals. Such arguments are notable for making an indirect case for the existence of universals by showing the extent of the difficulties that arise without them.

2.3.1 Russell's Regress Argument against the Denial of Universals

In *The Problems of Philosophy*, Russell (1912) presents a famous negative argument for the existence of universals by claiming that avoidance of universals leads to a vicious infinite regress. He describes the regress as follows:

> If we wish to avoid the universals *whiteness* and *triangularity*, we shall choose some particular patch of white or some particular triangle, and say that anything is white or a triangle if it has the right sort of resemblance to our chosen particular. But then the resemblance required will have to be a universal. Since there are many white things, the resemblance must hold between many pairs of particular white things; and this is the characteristic of a universal. It will be useless to say that there is a different resemblance for each pair, for then we shall have to say that these resemblances resemble each other, and thus at last we shall be forced to admit resemblance as a universal. The relation of resemblance, therefore, must be a true universal. And having been forced to admit this universal, we find that it is no longer worth while to invent difficult and unplausible theories to avoid the admission of such universals as whiteness and triangularity. (Russell 1912, p. 55)

Thus, if a nominalist wants to avoid postulating universals such as *whiteness* and *triangularity*, they need to find alternative ways of accounting for properties. One way of doing this is to pick out some particular, *d* – a particular patch of white or a particular triangle – and then take the properties of whiteness and triangularity to consist in the "right sort of resemblance" of particulars to the chosen paradigm, *d*. This position has come to be known as resemblance nominalism, or, more specifically, as paradigm resemblance nominalism. Now, as there are many white and triangular things, there will be many pairs of things resembling each other in the relevant way. Multiple recurrence is a characteristic of universals and if one wants to avoid admitting resemblance as a universal, a way to do this is by saying that there is a *different* resemblance for each pair (*a*,*d*), (*b*,*d*), (*c*,*d*), and so on – *r*(*a*,*d*), *r*(*b*,*d*), *r*(*c*,*d*), and so on. But if a nominalist says this, they find themselves again having to explain what makes all the resemblances, *r(a,d)*, *r(b,d)*, *r(c,d)*, and so forth, resemble each other. They may say that all of them resemble each other because each of them resembles some arbitrarily picked resemblance *r(x,d)*. In this way we get new pairs of resembling resemblances: (*r*[*a,d*], *r*[*x,d*]); (*r*[*b,d*], *r*[*x,d*]); (*r*[*c,d*], *r*[*x,d*]). And again, if in each case we ascribe the same resemblance, there arises a risk for the nominalist of admitting a universal into their system. Therefore, they have to say that each of the new pairs of resemblances are *different* particular resemblances, and so forth. The conclusion that Russell draws from this is that since the resistance to admit universals leads to an infinite regress of resemblance *relations*, a nominalist might as well accept the resemblance relation as a universal in the first place. And once one universal is admitted, why not let all of them in?

Immediately after his presentation of the regress argument for universals, Russell notes that Berkeley and Hume failed to appreciate the force of this argument because they thought of *qualities* rather than *relations* as exemplars of universals. For Russell, at this time, the opposite is the case: it is *relations* that are the main candidates for universals. Qualities can be treated, as the regress argument itself suggests, in terms of resemblance of one particular to another; relations, however, are irreducible. An attempt to rid oneself of relations leads to an infinite regress of further relations of *resemblance* or *likeness*. The argument thus proves very simply, according to Russell, that an ontology that admits of only particulars is flawed – it overlooks the fact that *relations* are ineliminable, and thus that universals are too.[6]

2.3.2 Against the Possibility of Paraphrasing Away the Reference to Universals

Another form of negative argument for universals that Armstrong presents originates from Pap (1959) and was reworked by Jackson (1977). It challenges the nominalist to translate the following two true statements about colors: (1) "Red resembles orange more than it resembles blue," and (2) "Red is a color."

A common nominalist paraphrase of the first of these statements would run something like: (1*) "For all particulars, *x*, *y*, and *z*, if *x* is red and *y* is orange and *z* is blue, then *x* resembles *y* more than *x* resembles *z*." But Pap points out that the translation proposed by the nominalist is *not* equivalent to the original statement since "*x* may resemble *z* more than *y* in other respects though *x* is red and *y* orange

[6] There is a lot more that can be said about the origin and impact of Russell's regress. For a further discussion, see Cargile (2003), Rodriguez-Pereyra (2004), and Perović (2015). There is also an important discussion about what makes for a vicious regress in Nolan (2001).

and *z* blue" (Pap 1959, p. 334). In other words, ordinary particulars *x*, *y*, and *z* will have other characteristics besides color. For instance, let *x* be a red cube, *y* an orange sphere, and *z* a blue sphere; in this case, the truth of statement (1) will stand unaffected whereas the translation (1*) turns out to be false.

At this point a nominalist can try rephrasing statement (1) in a way that specifies the respects of resemblance involved; Pap suggests something like: (1**) "For all particulars, *x*, *y*, and *z*, if *x* is red and *y* is orange and *z* is blue, then *x* resembles *y* in respect of color more than *x* resembles *z* in respect of color." The problem with this translation, Armstrong argues, is that "resemblance in respect of color" seems to refer to a four-term relation holding between *x*, *y*, *z*, and color – an option hardly attractive to nominalists, since they do not wish to be committed to relational universals any more than they want to be committed to property universals. Moreover, this paraphrase seems to introduce a reference to an additional universal – *color*. A better paraphrase would probably be: (1***) "For all particulars, *x*, *y* and *z*, if *x* is red and *y* is orange and *z* is blue, then *x colour-resembles y* more than *x colour-resembles z*" (Armstrong 1978, p. 59). Here, in place of "resemblance in respect of color," which seems to refer potentially to universal *color*, we have a predicate "color-resembles" which might avoid such commitment if it is taken to be a primitive predicate. But then concerns arise as to whether such a predicate is indeed sufficiently conceptually simple to be treated as a primitive and how it is to be distinguished from other resemblance predicates such as, say, shape-resemblance, temperature-resemblance, and so on. All of these resemblances are distinct – but in virtue of what?, challenges the realist.

Statement (2) "Red is a color" poses difficulties as well. One suggestion is to try and translate it along the lines of (1*), that is, as (2*): "For all particulars, *x*, if *x* is red, then *x* is colored." It is clear that (2) entails (2*) but in order for the translation to be successful the reverse has to be true as well. To test whether (2*) does entail (2), Jackson (1977) proposed consideration of an analogous case, the case of statement (3*): "For all particulars, *x*, if *x* is red, then *x* is extended." (3*) is a true statement; in fact, it appears to be a necessary truth like (2*). It seems, then, that if (2*) entails (2), then analogously, (3*) should entail (3): "Red is an extension." But (3) is clearly false. This, according to Jackson, and Armstrong who follows him, proves that (2) says something *more* than (2*) and that the nominalist hasn't managed to capture in their translation that *extra* something which (2) seems to express. In Jackson's words:

> If red's being a color were nothing more than a matter of every red thing necessarily being colored, then red's being a shape and an extension would be nothing more than the fact that necessarily every red thing is shaped and

> extended. And red is not a shape and not an extension. It seems that "Red is a color" says, as realists maintain, something about red not reducible to something about red things. (Jackson 1977, p. 427)

Of course, one need not take these arguments from the lack of adequate paraphrases of apparent references to universals as demonstrating anything more than a quirk of language. Namely, one may very well acknowledge that our ordinary language contains apparent references to universals that cannot be easily eliminated without loss of meaning, while at the same time maintaining that such a feature of language should not be seen as ontologically significant.

It's important to bear in mind that not one of the arguments discussed in this section is put forward as a decisive argument for universals. These arguments are presented here in order to illustrate what a *cumulative* case for one ontological category – the category of universals – looks like. It's inevitably a partial story, as some arguments can be replaced with others, perhaps more compelling ones. The "one-over-many" argument plays an important role in the overall story being told. Plato thought of it as an obviously decisive argument for universals, but contemporary metaphysicians today rarely think of it that way. The reconstruction of Armstrong's version of the argument was meant to show the different places where other philosophers might disagree and dispute the need to introduce the category of universals, and appeal to other categories and explanations in their stead.

3 Some Desiderata for a Promising System of Ontological Categories

Drawing on the case study of universals from Section 2, this section discusses some theoretical desiderata for building a promising system of ontological categories. The first desideratum is to make sure that the metaphysical question or problem that the ontological entity is introduced to address is well-stated and motivated. This, as we will see, requires taking special care to avoid engaging with metaphysical pseudo-problems. I then describe considerations of ontological and ideological economy that tend to guide philosophers in their theory-building. I also discuss the distinction between simple and more complex ontological entities, and the widely held assumption that fundamentality and simplicity go hand in hand in a metaphysical explanation. Sections 3.2.5 and 3.2.6 engage with the meta-theoretical considerations about the relationship between ontological entities, categories, and roles. Drawing on Oliver (1996), I make a case for characterizing ontological categories by appeal to ontological roles they play in solving certain metaphysical problems. I believe that this characterization best accommodates the piecemeal, revisionary, bottom-up approach that I advocate.

3.1 Motivating the Question and Steering Clear of Pseudo-Problems

In Section 2, we saw the category of universals introduced primarily through the "one-over-many" argument. We saw that Plato arrived at the conclusion of the argument – his introduction of Forms – very quickly, whereas Armstrong's development of the argument was a bit more gradual and careful. The crucial steps in Armstrong's version of the argument are to assert that there is a Moorean fact of sameness of type and then to require that this apparent fact be further explained.

Realists and trope theorists take this task on – the former attempting to provide an explanation by appeal to universals, while the latter appeal to tropes and their mutual resemblance. The question "what makes for genuine resemblance between this piece of paper and this table?" would thus, for a realist, be that they both share one and the same universal of *rectangularity*, whereas trope theorists would say that they each have a distinct trope of rectangularity, r_1 and r_2, and that the resemblance between these two tropes requires no further explanation or grounding.

Class nominalists resist the demand for an explanation of resemblance and take it to be a primitive and unanalyzable predicate which applies to natural classes of particulars. As Lewis forcefully puts it, "not every account is an analysis!" Taking certain facts as primitive and unanalyzed, according to him, is still a way of making room for them in one's ontology.

I have taken the debate surrounding universals as itself a paradigmatic case of the way that the introduction of a new and distinct ontological category often proceeds. Of course, each debate has its own individual features, parameters, distinctions, and so on. But there are definite similarities among them, too. Consider, for example, the debate about whether or not we ought to be committed to causal relations, or bare particulars, or states of affairs, or temporal parts, and so on. In each of these cases the starting point is a certain target phenomenon, a certain undeniable "Moorean fact." It seems that when I push this table I *cause* it to move – what is this due to? Is there something corresponding to my sense that there is a causal relation between the two events? It looks as if exact duplicates such as, say, these two qualitatively identical erasers, can share all of the same qualities but still be *two*. What makes for distinctness between exactly similar objects? All sorts of things seem to remain the same, even through changes in properties: How can something change and yet remain the same?

In all of these cases, the starting point is a demand for an analysis of a certain undeniable "Moorean fact." A refusal to provide an analysis is, of course, an option, but certain dialectical circumstances might make such a choice harder or easier. If the majority view in a given ontological debate is that a problem is an important one and in definite need of being addressed, then it becomes a problem which is hard to ignore. Not engaging becomes in itself a controversial stance, one which needs to be explained and justified. In addition, if a number of prominent philosophers have recognized the problem and tackled it, this adds to the pressure and makes it difficult to disengage with the problem as stated. At the same time, if a certain philosophical problem is considered to be a serious one only by a handful of philosophers, it is easier not to be drawn into a dispute whose significance many do not recognize. Thus, which question is considered to be a compulsory one in a given ontological debate is often, to a greater degree than metaphysicians would like to admit, a circumstantial matter.

Regardless of circumstances and philosophical trends and fashions, what helps make an ontological question or problem a compulsory and an enduring one is the way it is stated. The statement of it should be clear and well-motivated. The theses that give rise to the problem should be made explicit, as well as any controversial underlying assumptions presupposed by those theses. Formulating the problem as a puzzle that needs solving can also be very helpful, as it often sheds light on assumptions that cannot all be held together.[7] The risks of not stating and motivating the problem properly are great – for we might find ourselves addressing a metaphysical pseudo-problem and postulating entities aimed at addressing it. By a metaphysical pseudo-problem, I understand the sort of problem that in its statement commits the fallacy of a complex question. Such a fallacy is committed when, in posing the question or problem, one tacitly takes for granted controversial assumptions which others would not grant if made explicit; or assumptions which are simply untrue; or assumptions which assume a false dichotomy. As a result, in response to the question so posed, answers, too, are severely restricted by those tacit assumptions – in other words, if one wants to engage a certain problem or question, one seems to have no option but to accept those very same tacit and unsubstantiated assumptions which were presupposed by the question.

A nonphilosophical example of a complex question is someone asking, for instance: "Did you poison your husband on Tuesday or on Wednesday?" This question makes three assumptions that need to be established rather than merely assumed: the first one is that the person addressed has a husband; the second one is that the person has poisoned their husband; and the third one is that they did it on one of the two days mentioned. If this person replied, "But I did not poison my husband!" or "I don't have a husband" or "I have a husband and he is alive and well," one wouldn't be addressing the question as posed.

---

[7] Sider (Conee and Sider 2007) provides a nice example of this in his articulation of the puzzle of coinciding objects.

I take one of the paradigmatic metaphysical pseudo-problems to be: "Why is there something rather than nothing?" This question is often taken to be one of the most fundamental metaphysical problems; it captures the wonder one feels about there being a universe at all. One way of arriving at the question is via a subtraction argument. The thinking is as follows: it seems as if there need not have been any contingent existents – this table, this chair, this office, me, you, and so on. It seems that any number of contingent beings might not have existed. An entire universe, which also seems to be a contingent being, might not have existed. In fact, it seems quite possible that there might not have been anything at all. So how come – *what is the reason* – for there being something rather than nothing?

Metaphysicians are usually quick to dismiss as plausible any causal answer to this question. As Conee (Conee and Sider 2007) points out, the question is not concerned with *physical causes* of the origin of the universe; that is, it is not after the causal story that explains the big bang. Rather, it is after something more general and more fundamental. The idea is that even if there were a satisfactory answer regarding what caused the big bang, the metaphysical question would still remain: What caused the big bang? And why was there such a cause rather than nothing? The answer to the metaphysical version of "Why is there something rather than nothing?," we are told, is not meant to take anything for granted – no physical laws of any kind, no objects, nothing at all.

Historically, the most popular answers to this question have appealed to necessitarianism of some kind. The answer to the question would then take the form: "the reason why there is something rather than nothing is because there are beings that *have to be*, that exist out of necessity." But arguments in favor of necessary beings – whether it be a god, or a number, or a proposition – are problematic in many ways. Further still, it is often pointed out that even if we were to find compelling arguments for the existence of certain necessary beings, the existence of contingents would be open to the same type of question as the initial one, namely: "Why are there these contingent beings rather than none (or some others)?"

It is not my aim here to engage in any depth with the various answers that have been given to this question. I just want to pinpoint aspects of the question which, I believe, make it a poorly motivated "pseudo-problem" and thus one of those questions that is not compulsory.

First, the phrasing of the question is such that it seems to privilege nothing over something. To ask "why is there something rather than nothing?" presupposes that "nothing" is a default natural state, as opposed to a something, which is taken to be surprising and in need of explanation. But, for the question to be a fruitful one, the naturalness of the nothing state needs to be established, not merely assumed. Grünbaum (2009) has argued that the assumption of "the ontological spontaneity of nothingness"(SoN) finds its historical origin in the Christian doctrine. Considering *nothing* as a natural state seems to be presupposed by the doctrine that mandates that an all-powerful being acts as a creative (and maintaining) cause of the universe. He also notes that SoN has been defended by Leibniz and Swinburne as an ontologically and conceptually simpler alternative. But it is not at all clear that ontological simplicity is more spontaneously realized in the absence of the overriding cause. Thus, proponents of the question "why is there something rather than nothing?" need to provide further arguments for SoN if the question is to be posed in this way.

There is an additional difficulty with the question when it comes to "nothing"; it is very unclear how we ought to characterize it, so that it actually presents a genuine ontological possibility. One suggestion might be to think of it as a negative fact; but this only leads to more questions: Is it a negative fact of totality or a totality of infinitely many negative facts? How are we to think of negative facts – as absences of facts, or negative instantiations of properties by particulars, or as instantiations of negative universals, or in some other way entirely? And so on and so forth. It might be hard to address these questions, but if we are engaging with a genuine problem, rather than a pseudo-problem, some clarity about these needs to be established.

Finally, the "why is there something" part of the question seems to be relying on a version of the Principle of Sufficient Reason (PSR). According to PSR, "for each thing that exists or obtains, there is an explanation of its existence, a reason that it exists" (Della Rocca 2010, p. 1). Now, for PSR to present support and motivation for the "why is there something" part of the question, the sort of explanation it is after needs to be made clearer. Explanations of existence are difficult to evaluate. On the one hand, proponents of PSR are usually quick to reject the idea that they are after a causal story of some kind. On the other hand, it is not quite clear what sort of explanatory story is sought in this context. Is it an explanation of how come there is a *specific* something? If so, explanations will vary depending on the existent in question. (There will be different – possibly again, causal – stories for dinosaurs, persons, artifacts, and yet a different one again for abstract particulars or universals etc.). Perhaps the PSR in this case is after some kind of a *global explanation* of an entire universe; but it is not clear how global explanations are meant to work. (Are they made up of many partial explanations of individual existents or are they supposed to be an explanation of a whole universe? If it's the latter, then one needs to establish first the existence of such an "entity" as an "entire universe" as something over and above all of its parts, and as something in need of a different sort of explanation than all of its parts.)

To briefly summarize, the question "why is there something rather than nothing?," without further clarification, is an example of a pseudo-problem. That is, it uses terms such as "nothing" which need an ontological account and clarification. It also takes the form of a complex question, insofar as it seems to privilege "nothing" as a default state, and this sort of assumption needs significant defense in its own right. And, finally, the question seems to tacitly rely on a certain form of PSR, a principle which – as I have suggested – itself needs to be defended, especially in its application in this context.

To be sure, complex questions might be useful and revelatory in some contexts – such as when used as an interrogation technique by investigators, or by prosecutors in courtrooms. Such questions may even prove to be rhetorically effective when employed by psychologists; for instance, a therapist might ask: "I wonder what prevents you from acting upon your decision?" In fact, such questions might act as a useful shortcut whenever it is assumed that there is a shared background context of discussion. But in a philosophical context, where the context of discussion has *not* been established and where the tacit assumptions are not shared and properly argued for, complex questions are extremely problematic and give rise to pseudo-problems. In such cases, it is paramount that the assumptions that are being made are brought to light and examined, as well as whether they are properly supported and whether there is still a good question to be asked once this work has been done.

This sort of work is particularly important in the context of ontological discussions. These kinds of discussion are foundational, and if one ends up introducing ontological categories hastily and on shaky and unchecked foundations, it will reverberate throughout one's metaphysical system.

Before moving on to the next section, I will offer a couple of clarifications. First, I wouldn't want someone to take away from discussion this that I am advocating that each and every assumption in one's system needs to be thoroughly supported and that I do not allow for so-called primitives in one's theory. On the contrary, as we will in Section 3.2, I acknowledge that such primitives are necessary; the stress here is only on making such primitives explicit, especially in the formulation of what one wants to pose as a "compulsory" metaphysical problem. Second, I do not want to imply that in order to avoid stating pseudo-problems, philosophers must at all cost state philosophical problems in some perfectly "neutral" way. Here too, I suggest that transparency is the best policy. One might, just like Armstrong in advocating for universals, provide opinionated introductions to a favored philosophical problem in order to draw readers in and make them "feel" the pull of the problem for themselves. But in doing so, one must also be careful to make one's philosophical opinions and preferences explicit.

3.2 Ontological Categories and Theory-Building

3.2.1 Ontology versus Ideology

Once one has followed the suggestions in Section 3.1, and hopefully managed to motivate and state the metaphysical problem reasonably well – perhaps as in the Armstrongian version of the "one over many" – there is a great deal more to do.

Section 2 showed how one metaphysical problem can be addressed in a number of ways, and introduced different types of entities. A useful way of thinking about this is in terms of ontological roles and role-fillers. An entity that gets introduced into one's ontology is meant to fill a certain role in the overall theory. As we saw, universals were introduced to ground the sharing and having of genuine properties; tropes were introduced to ground the having of properties, but the resemblance between distinct tropes was considered not to require a further common ground. Thus, the initial decision about which categories are introduced depends on what sort of phenomenon one wants to provide an explanation for, and what sort of entity the philosopher deems to be best equipped for that job.

Then, when evaluating a metaphysical theory, philosophers often appeal to Quine's (1951) distinction between ontology and ideology. Ontology refers to the entities that the theory claims exist; ideology refers, somewhat vaguely, to ideas, concepts, and explanations provided by a theory. According to this distinction, discussion about virtues of a given ontology, descriptions of different ontological roles, characterizations of different types of entities, the sorting of different entities into different categories, and so on all fall within the realm of ideology.

When comparing metaphysical theories, philosophers consider how they fare with respect to both ontological and ideological economy. A theory is ontologically economical if it introduces only a small number of fundamental entities. This idea captures nicely the gist of Occam's razor, that is, the famous medieval dictum that prescribes that "we should not postulate entities beyond necessity." On the other hand, a theory is ideologically economical if it has very few unanalyzable primitive predicates. Philosophers tend to think of both of these types of economy as desirable and as enhancing a theory's explanatory power: an explanation that is ideologically simple and elegant and that postulates only a small number of entities is an ideal one. But there is often a certain amount of trade-off between ideological economy and ontological economy; that is, explanations that appeal to only a small number of primitive predicates often end up postulating a greater number of entities, and vice versa – explanations which postulate only a few fundamental entities will often end up with a greater number of complicated predicates.

The trade-off between ideological and ontological economy could be seen in Section 2 in the discussion on different approaches to properties and relations.

Postulating universals alongside particulars inflates the realist's ontology more than, say, a one-category ontology of tropes or Lewis's ontology of particulars, and classes of actual and possible particulars. At the same time, universals were introduced as entities whose role was to account for the having and sharing of genuine properties between particulars; thus a boost in ontology came with a prima facie gain in ideological economy. Trope theorists and class and resemblance nominalists, on the other hand, found themselves admitting more of the complex primitive predicates than realists, such as a primitive predicate of resemblance or, in the case of class nominalists, a contrastive and variably polyadic predicate of naturalness.

Lewis (1973, p. 87) has made a distinction between two types of ontological economy: the *qualitative* economy and the *quantitative* economy. Qualitative economy is measured by the number of *kinds* of postulated entities; quantitative economy refers to the sheer number of *entities*, of any kind, postulated by a theory. Lewis has argued that only qualitative economy matters – a position that allows him to claim that his ontology is more economical than the realist's. Rodriguez-Pereyra (2002), on the other hand, argues that both sorts of economy matter but that *qualitative* economy "takes precedence" over the quantitative one. Thus, for example, a boost in ontology brought about by admitting concrete *possibilia* into one's ontology would reflect a quantitative gain, but not a qualitative one (since one would continue to have just particulars in one's ontology). The worry then might be whether such an application of the distinction is rather ad hoc and the commitment to infinite concrete possible individuals such as talking donkeys, flying pigs, unicorns, gods, and so on is not just more of the same plain-old particulars. A challenger could perhaps argue that concrete *possibilia* are in fact a different *kind* of entity altogether. I won't try to settle this dispute here; it is just important to keep in mind that there is less consensus about this aspect of metaphysical methodology than one might assume.

Assessing ideological economy is similarly challenging – it is both important but also controversial. It is not just complex primitive predicates that are found to be undesirable but, more generally, any kind of convoluted metaphysical explanation and theory. What philosophers are after, ideally, are theories that are clear, elegant, and fruitful. Such theories should only take as unanalyzable concepts that are clear and self-evident and proceed in a systematic and gradual way to explain the more complex components of the system in terms of the more simple ones. The fruitfulness of the theory is also very important and is measured by how well it explains the phenomenon it was intended to explain, and whether it can be reapplied successfully to other areas of inquiry.

Let me illustrate this last point with the following example. When a realist introduces universals to ground resemblance between distinct particulars, it may not look good for the fruitfulness of the theory if resemblance between universals cannot receive the same type of treatment. Examples of resemblance between universals are as follows: *crimson* resembles *vermilion* in being *red*, *triangularity* is more like *quadrilaterality* than it is like *circularity*, and both *triangularity* and *circularity* resemble in being *shapes*. But analyzing these resemblances among universals by appeal to universals is highly problematic. If resembling universals are themselves taken to instantiate second-order universals, it would seem to imply that they would themselves have to be instances of those universals. And yet this can't be, since universal properties of *triangularity* and *circularity* are not themselves *instances* of shapes; that is, they are not themselves shaped. Similarly, *crimson* and *vermilion* are not themselves *red*. Take, again, *triangularity* and *circularity*; these two property universals resemble in that they are both *shapes*. But they also differ as *shapes*. Armstrong himself recognized that this was not a tenable view, since "things cannot differ in the respect in which they are identical" (Armstrong 1978, p. 106). Thus, rather than have one and the same thing serve as the ontological ground of sameness *and* difference between two other entities, what is needed are distinct entities one (or more) of which will serve as a resemblance-maker, and the other which will serve as a difference-maker. *Being a shape* fails on both accounts: it is neither specific enough to be able to capture a resemblance-order that exists between different shapes, nor specific enough to account for what makes different shapes distinct. Resemblance between universals thus has to receive a different account entirely from that which applies to resemblance between particulars and this, arguably, does not look good for the fruitfulness of the realist's ideology.

3.2.2 Complex and Simple Entities

In metaphysical theory-building, there are entities that are taken to belong to the most fundamental ontological categories and that serve as the building blocks of one's ontology; and then there are entities that are more complex, composed of the more fundamental entities. For example, particulars and universals can be taken as the most fundamental ontological building blocks, while states of affairs can be seen as the more complex entities that are made up of these two.

The more complex entities should not be introduced ad hoc; they, too, require a well-motivated argument in favor of their postulation. Armstrong, for example, produces a truthmaker argument for states of affairs. This argument rests on the assumption that all truths require an ontological ground, that is, something in the world that makes them true. He then goes on to make a case that, truthmakers for truths about particular things having properties, and standing in relations to other things, need to appeal to states of affairs. He thinks the truth of the sentence "this chalk is white," or the form "a is F," cannot be made true by *a* all by itself construed as what he calls a "thin particular" (since *a* does not include all its properties); nor does it suffice to appeal to a universal, *F*, by itself. A pair (*a*, *F*) won't do either, he claims, since both *a* and *F* could exist without it being the case that *a is F.* Thus, according to Armstrong, the correct truthmaker and ontological ground for such truths has to be *the state of affairs a's* being *F*; such a state of affairs is made up of the particular *a* and the universal *F*, but is also seen as something over and above the two.

Arguments for complex entities face most of the same challenges as arguments for the simpler ones. Philosophers might disagree with the assumptions of the argument presented (in the example just given, one might dispute the truthmaker approach itself based on, say, an alternative theory of truth, or how the truthmaker argument applies in this context). Or, they may disagree about whether the introduced complex entity is in fact needed, that is, whether the explanatory role it is introduced to fill warrants the ontological inflation that takes place (e.g. one might dispute that the truthmaker argument requires states of affairs to fill the particular truthmaking role). They can further disagree about which ontological category the new entity belongs to, that is, whether it falls within the existing categories or whether it is in a new sui generis category (when it comes to states of affairs, one might wonder if they themselves are particulars, universals, or something else). But the new aspect that complex entities bring into view are questions about the nature of the relationship that the complex has to the simpler entities that constitute it (in the case of states of affairs this has been a particularly fraught debate, since these entities do not abide by the model of mereological constitution).

3.2.3 Fundamentality and Primitives

As noted in the previous section, metaphysicians commonly take complexity of an entity to imply that such an entity has constituents, while simple entities, by contrast, have no further constituents. States of affairs are thus assumed to be constituted of particulars and universals, and in this sense they are indeed complex entities. For many, this also means that such entities cannot be fundamental.[8] The background assumption here is that fundamentality and simplicity go hand in hand. But this assumption itself must be treated with caution, since there are different ways in which an entity can be taken to be fundamental.[9]

[8] Bradley (1910) famously puzzled over Russell's suggestion that an entity can be fundamental *and* have constituents. Many more philosophers after him have had a similar thought.

[9] For an in-depth treatment of the concept of fundamentality, see Tahko (2018).

A great deal of the recent literature in metaphysics has been dedicated to the concepts of ontological dependence, metaphysical explanation, and grounding.[10] All too often it is assumed that metaphysical explanation and ontological dependence go hand in hand; the thought is that the metaphysical explanation will follow the chains of ontological dependence, where the latter is frequently characterized in terms of existential dependence of entities and in terms of relationship of constitution. In its turn, then, ontological dependence is characterized as an ontological analogue of metaphysical explanation – thus, the "ontologically fundamental" entities are considered to be the ones that are fundamental for explanatory purposes.

Where the two notions become completely indistinguishable is in loose metaphysical talk of entities *explaining* a certain phenomenon. But I believe this to be a misguided way of talking. For how might an entity do any explaining? It seems to me more correct to say that *we* explain phenomena by appeal to certain ontological categories or entities; entities themselves don't explain anything. Of course, an appeal to certain entities and their features might make our explanations simpler and easier to follow, while other explanations might seem more complex and difficult. But regardless of how the explanations might go, the entities are doing no more explaining than, say, a virus or a bacterium itself explains the disease that it causes.[11]

Once we dissociate the simplicity/complexity of an entity from the simplicity/complexity of the explanation that appeals to such an entity, we can see that one need not associate the notion of fundamentality with an entity's simplicity. Indeed, it seems useful to distinguish between at least the following three senses in which an entity can be taken to be fundamental: *constitutive*, *explanatory*, and *existential*. Although some of these types of fundamentality end up picking out the same entities, they need not do so, for they are quite different. I have elsewhere suggested the following characterizations:[12]

Constitutive fundamentality. An entity *e* is *constitutively* more fundamental than entity *e** iff *e* is a constituent of *e**, where constitution is construed broadly to include mereological *and* nonmereological forms of constitution.

Explanatory fundamentality. An entity *e* is *explanatorily* more fundamental than entity *e** iff the definition or a characterization of *e***'s ontological role

[10] See, for instance, Cameron (2008), Correia (2008), Schaffer (2012), Tahko and Lowe (2020).

[11] An anonymous reviewer has pointed out that some philosophers such as Lowe (2018) do indeed find that essences explain metaphysically. I suspect that what is meant by this claim is simply that an appeal to the essential properties of an entity helps us understand its nature.

[12] See Perović (2016).

cannot be made without reference to *e*, where *e* is either taken as an explanatory primitive or can be characterized independently from *e**.

Existential fundamentality. An entity *e* is *existentially* more fundamental than entity *e** iff *e** cannot exist without *e*, whereas *e* can exist without *e**.

These distinctions help characterize the relationships between simple and complex entities in more nuanced ways. Applied to our case study of universals, particulars, and states of affairs, they give us the following conceptual possibilities. First, particulars and universals appear to be *constitutively* more fundamental than Armstrongian states of affairs; tropes are *constitutively* more fundamental than, say, bundles of tropes, and so on. But, at the same time, a realist like Armstrong could make a case that facts or states of affairs are *explanatorily* more fundamental than particulars and the universals that make them up; states of affairs can be characterized via the truthmaking argument – they are the entities that make sentences about the having and sharing of properties true. One might think that what makes up such entities is a further question that may have different answers depending on the type of ontology one embraces. From this we can start to see how *constitutive* and *explanatory* fundamentality might come apart and pick out different entities.

Existential fundamentality also need not match up with constitutive fundamentality. Some entities might be constituents of other more constitutively complex ones, but both simple and complex ones might be mutually existentially dependent upon one another. For instance, in our case study, all three entities – particulars, universals, and states of affairs – seem to be on a par when it comes to existential dependence. None can exist without the others. Particulars cannot exist but in states of affairs; universals cannot exist uninstantiated and thus in states of affairs; and, for an immanent realist, states of affairs cannot exist without particulars and universals.

Existential fundamentality can be further refined in a number of ways. It can be useful to distinguish, for instance, between the type of existential dependence that holds between a given circle, *c*, and its essential property of *extendedness*, and a circle, *c*, and its nonessential property of *redness*. It seems as if *c* cannot exist without it being extended and circular, but it *can* exist without it being red (it might be some other color). Various more fine-grained types of existential fundamentality are discussed in detail by Tahko and Lowe (2020).

To sum up, these distinctions help us see how some entities might indeed be constitutively complex but also, in a different sense, fundamental and unanalyzable. For instance, states of affairs appear to be existentially as fundamental as particulars and universals; they are constitutively complex (and thus *not* fundamental in this sense); and they may even be seen as explanatorily more fundamental than both particulars and universals.

Relating to concepts of simplicity and fundamentality is the concept of a "primitive" in one's theory. Metaphysical literature frequently loosely appeals to the use of "primitives" whenever a certain type of entity or concept cannot be further explained. But here, too, just as in the case of fundamentality, we need to be careful. Postulated entities, strictly speaking, are not "primitive"; they are simple or fundamental in one of the above senses. Predicates and concepts, on the other hand, when they cannot be further explained and analyzed, are taken to be primitives of the theory. For instance, in one's theory of time, one might treat the passage of time as a primitive; that is, it is taken as something that cannot receive further analysis or a noncircular explanation (i.e., an explanation that does not refer to the very concept it sets out to explain). This does not mean, however, that there is nothing more to be said about the primitive. In fact, one would hope that different descriptions and characterizations *can* be afforded. The very idea is to take something intuitively compelling as a primitive notion that one would hope to be able to describe further; but because it is explanatorily fundamental, it cannot be further *defined* or *explained away* in terms of something more explanatorily simple.

There are, of course, gray areas, and even strong philosophical disagreements about whether or not a certain concept or predicate makes for a convincing primitive. For example, we have seen Lewis argue for the notion of a natural property, or his notion of a contrastive and polyadic predicate of resemblance to be taken as a primitive. In such contexts, philosophers appeal to primitives as a way of signaling that explanation does not go any further, that one has reached the bottom line of a theorist's ideology.

And yet philosophical inquiry and the need for analysis cannot be hushed so easily. Philosophers have been known to put pressure on concepts that other philosophers have taken to be primitive and unanalyzable. Take, for example, relations. External relations, such as spatial and temporal relations (e.g. "two feet apart," "to the left of," "preceding") have been taken by many philosophers to be unproblematic. At one point, Russell (1911) thought that relations might just be the ultimate constituents of reality and that everything might indeed be reducible to bundles of universals and relations among them. Other philosophers have been suspicious of relations, finding them to be extremely puzzling. F. H. Bradley (1893), for instance, famously argued that relations conceived as external lead to an infinite regress, while relations conceived as internal, that is, as grounded in their relata (e.g. "taller than," "greater than") also lead to contradictions and an infinite regress of relations. Regress arguments were a commonly used philosophical tool at the turn of the twentieth century. They were often generated in order to show that using a certain concept or entity to explain a certain phenomenon was somehow insufficient; more entities or concepts of the same kind would need to be introduced, ad infinitum, never arriving at an ultimate reductive explanation. Bradley's regress arguments against relations attempted to make just that point – he wanted to demonstrate that relations could not fill the relating task in a satisfactory way and that more and more relations would need to keep being introduced to do the job. The assumption that generated the relational regresses was that relations could not relate, that they were simply not up to the task. Thus, the deeper dispute about relations had to do with the question whether they can actually fulfill the ontological role assigned to them. Once it became clear that Bradley's deeper concern was that relations could not relate, while Russell thought that they could, there was not much of a dispute left. The two philosophers found themselves at an impasse. Bradley (1911) expressed his final concern to Russell by asking him to explain further "*how* relations relate." This sort of question has been echoed by contemporary metaphysicians suspicious of relations' ability to relate. Some philosophers respond to this with the claim that this is just what relations do; others find such an answer deeply frustrating and unsatisfactory. The former then insist that they have an entity in their arsenal that fulfills a certain role, and that the way that it fulfills that role is not something up for dispute; how an entity fulfills its role is a primitive of a theory. Opponents, on the other hand, stress that the "how" question is a compulsory one, and that without addressing it adequately the entire matter is shrouded in mystery.

As this example illustrates, what makes for a good primitive concept in one's theory is often a controversial matter. Intuitiveness is a notoriously unreliable guide in philosophy. Among philosophers, intuitions are highly variable and change over time. In addition, one needs to be careful about how far to push the "why" and "how" questions in philosophy. What seems to power questions of the type "how does a relation relate?" is reasoning similar to that in the PSR. This principle states, roughly, that everything must have "a sufficient reason." But this, of course, is too vague. The "sufficient reason" sometimes refers to an explanation of a certain phenomenon, at other times to a physical cause, and at yet other times to ontological ground. These are all clearly very different ways of articulating a "reason" for something. What they all have in common, and what I assume the PSR tries to capture, is the sense that there ought to be some sort of explanation for every thing/occurrence/phenomenon. This kind of search for an explanation well encapsulates what lies at the core of our attempts to understand ourselves, the world around us, and our place in such a world. It is the sort of wonder that has led to various scientific discoveries, both large and small. But if the PSR is only meant to capture something as vague as "human sense of wonder" and "search for explanations," then it is indeed too broad and vague to do any real philosophical work.

We can be in favor of searching for explanations of a variety of phenomena and also recognize that some concepts should be taken as primitive. We can appreciate the importance of wonder and curiosity, while recognizing that some questions are better formulated and more fruitful than others; and, indeed, that some questions might just be confused, misplaced, or even give rise to pseudo-problems. In doing fundamental ontology, metaphysicians sometimes have a difficult time walking the thin line between rightful questioning of certain fundamental assumptions, on the one hand, and risking sounding like a small child who won't stop asking "why" of any explanation they are provided with, on the other. Unfortunately, PSR is of no help in distinguishing between the two sides of the line. If it is to capture a particular kind of request for an explanation, it should be made more specific. If it is to remain broad and vague, it confers no particular weight or legitimacy to its demands for reasons and explanations.

3.2.4 Naturalistic Considerations

In providing reasons for postulating a certain kind of entity, some philosophers have appealed to naturalistic considerations. Armstrong has famously appealed to the Eleatic principle which dictates that one should only believe in entities that are causally efficacious. But causal efficacy can be understood in at least two ways. One way is to include entities that play an important role within a causal explanation; another way is to postulate entities that themselves must causally partake in the natural world. On the first interpretation, naturalism would come to encompass entities that need not themselves be causally efficacious and need not be part of the spatio-temporal physical world, but that nonetheless *feature* in explanations of such a world. Such entities might be numbers, propositions, universals, thoughts, and so on. This understanding of naturalness in ontology is probably too permissive and not what most philosophers are after when they talk about naturalistic ontology. But if interpret an appeal to naturalism as a way to include only entities that are themselves causally efficacious, this can seem both too restrictive and too vague. It can be seen as too restrictive in the sense that it might leave out too many entities that play an important explanatory role in a metaphysical theory – such as *possibilia*, substances, selves, and so forth – while at the same time not being causally efficacious in a straightforward way. The vagueness is also a problem – causal efficacy of an entity would need to be spelled out further; for instance, is causal efficacy to apply only to things or also their properties and, if so, which account of properties is presupposed? Armstrong, for example, believed that only scientific universals – those that feature in fundamental physics – should be allowed. But this, of course, potentially leaves many other perfectly good candidates out: universals from different sciences that are not fundamental physics as well as the category of universals itself seem to be left out of the picture. In any case, if appeal to naturalism is to play an important role in deciding which sorts of ontological entities one should admit, then at the very least one should make sure that the sense of "naturalism" is properly delineated, as well, of course, as the particular sense in which causal efficacy is to be understood in that philosopher's theory.

3.2.5 Ontological Categories, Entities, and Roles

The phrase "ontological categories" is commonly used to describe the most general *groupings* of everything that exists; "ontological entities," on the other hand, ordinarily refers to the entities that are taken to *fall under* those general groupings. When it comes to universals, the two terms are often used interchangeably. The reason, as we have seen, is that realists tend to introduce universals as the *type of entity* that itself sorts other entities into groups, as well as the entity that provides the ontological ground of resemblance between the distinct particulars within those groupings. These two roles that universals play has been present from their inception, and we have seen it on display in Section 2 in the way that Plato introduced his Forms.

But strictly speaking, the two terms can and do come apart, and should be kept separate. The term "ontological category" is mostly used to pick out a type of entity which has certain distinctive features, though those features need not be universals. This is something that nominalists and trope theorists are more accustomed to, since they do not admit universals to provide the ontological ground of genuine resemblances in nature. Instead, they tend to think of resemblance between such entities as holding due to those entities' natures, where the latter can be understood by appeal to, say, nonrepeatable property tropes.

Distinction between ontological categories and entities that fall under such categories is important to maintain for realists, as well. This is most clearly seen when examining the issue of the most general categories. To help explain the issue, I will utilize the determinate/determinable distinction introduced by Johnson (1921). Johnson outlined five main features of the relationship between determinate and determinable:

(1) if a particular has a determinable property, then it also has some determinate property that falls under that determinable (for instance, if *a* is *red*, it may not be *crimson* nor *scarlet* but it must be *some specific* shade of red; or if something has a shape, it must have a specific shape such as *rectangularity*);

(2) if a particular has a determinate property, then it also has the corresponding determinable property (if *a* is *crimson*, then it is automatically *red*);
(3) a particular cannot have more than one determinate property of a specific determinable at the same time (*a* cannot at once be *crimson* and *scarlet* all over, weigh *4 kg* and *5 kg*, be *triangular* and *quadrilateral*);
(4) the relationship between determinable and determinate is not to be confused with the relationship between species and genus (the definition of species involves *differentia* which is an independent property from genus, whereas in defining determinates there is no such independent property); and
(5) within a class of determinates that fall under the same determinable there are resemblances and these resemblances can be ordered (*scarlet* resembles *vermilion* more than it resembles *crimson*, for instance); this, however, is not the case with "highest" determinables.

As these features illustrate, determinate and determinable are introduced as fundamentally relational categories, defined in terms of one another. They are notions that do not seem to unequivocally fix their referents, since what is a determinate with respect to one determinable can itself often be a determinable with respect to another, "lower," determinate.

Now, when it comes to the most general groupings of entities – the most general categories – it might be tempting for a realist to appeal to *determinable universals* such as *having shape*, *being extended*, or perhaps even *being a universal* or *being an entity*. But the challenges for taking such high determinable properties to be universals are serious: one challenge has to do with what one should take the bearer of the higher-order determinable universal to be (should it be a particular or a first-order universal, and how should either of the two accounts be spelled out?); but the more pressing challenge in this context has to do with how undiscriminating such highly general determinables actually are. *Being extended, being a universal*, and *being an entity* appear to be too general for the role of resemblance-making; indeed, from that perspective, it doesn't seem right to think of them as universals at all.

I thus suggest that the best way to describe categories for realists, trope theorists, and nominalists alike, is by appeal to ontological roles. This approach was captured well by Oliver (1996), and I believe that such an approach most clearly acknowledges that coming up with categories of entities is not done outside of a specific metaphysical context. In metaphysics, we find many problems/puzzles that need to be solved, and it is in addressing such problems that the appeal to ontological categories plays an important part. When ontological categories and entities within them are charged with specific explanatory roles, their introduction can be properly motivated and critically assessed.

The assumptions present in the search for ontological categories, as well as the assessment of different category systems, become more transparent within such a framework. We can question, for instance, whether there is a need to introduce the category of universals or not, and whether the ontological role that universals are meant to fulfill needs to be filled, and if so, with what kind of entity.

The way in which one ontological role is characterized will in turn determine other ontological roles that need to be filled. For example, when universals are characterized as resemblance-makers, particulars tend to be characterized as distinctness-makers: they provide the ground of the multiplicity of numerically distinct entities. The need for a role of this kind can be gleaned by considering the problem of individuation. Namely, if the realist about universals wanted to just have universals in their ontology, they would have to analyze particulars such as, say, an apple, by appeal to property universals like *juiciness*, *redness, sweetness*, and so on. Thus, a particular red and ripe apple would just be a bundle of property universals. But it quickly becomes apparent that there can be two or more exact duplicates that share all of the same property universals – two or more apples that have exactly the same *juiciness*, *redness*, and *sweetness*. What then makes it so that there are two (or more) distinct apples rather than just one? If one is committed only to universals, and universals are seen as repeatable entities that are wholly present in each of their instances, what metaphysically distinguishes one bundle of universals from another exactly resembling one? What prevents all of the apples that exactly resemble one another in the universals they instantiate from collapsing into just one bundle of universals? These questions motivate many realists to explicitly postulate two categories of entities – particulars *and* universals – rather than just universals. Particulars' role is thus to help solve the problem of individuation by providing an ontological ground of distinctness of entities. Particulars can, of course, play additional roles and be used to solve further problems, similar to how we saw universals supported by further arguments in Section 2. For instance, one might appeal to them as what underlies change in properties through time, what bears properties and stands in relations to other particulars, and so on.

We can see that the main ontological roles that particulars and universals are assigned to fill seem well-defined and exclusive; when it comes to resemblance-making and difference-making, entities typically fall into one of the two categories – they are either particulars or universals, not both at once. This is not to say that a more complex entity – such as a state of affairs – cannot *contain* both of these entities. This is indeed how states of affairs are understood: they are entities made up of a particular having a certain universal (*Fa*), or two or more particulars standing in a certain relation (*aRb*). But a state of affairs is ordinarily itself conceived as a nonrepeatable entity – a particular. Armstrong referred to this feature of states of affairs as "victory of particularity."

The same entity can be cross-categorized – indeed, it often will belong to a number of different ontological categories. Take, for example, an abstract universal *being a prime number*; this entity belongs to a category of universals as well as to a category of abstract entities. Or take the event of *Lulu's 9th birthday party* – this event can be seen as a nonrepeatable entity that falls under the category of "particular," but is also a concrete spatio-temporal event with a certain duration. And so on and so forth. Different metaphysical systems will make different choices about what they take to be the most fundamental ontological categories as well as what they take to be the ontological entities within those categories, and what their features are. For instance, a universal will be seen as an abstract entity by some, while it will be understood as a concrete spatio-temporal entity by others. An event might be seen as a sum of static temporal parts by proponents of the four-dimensional approach to persistence, while it will be understood as an intrinsically dynamic temporally extended state of affairs by some proponents of the three-dimensional approach to persistence.

Not only will there be differences among the entities admitted and their characterizations, but the way that distinctions between entities are drawn up will vary as well. Most philosophers believe that ontological roles need to be defined neatly and exclusively, so that there is no confusion about which entities are introduced to fill which roles. Property universals ground resemblance between what appears to be sameness of qualities between particulars; particulars make for numerical distinctness; relations relate; and so on. But these neat divisions of roles, though desirable, are not always carried out. Sometimes the roles are found to be not defined well enough and/or are not exclusive enough.[13] Take, for instance, Russell's (1911, 1992) characterization of relations as entities that can fill *two* roles, depending on the situation they are in: in some situations they relate, in others they are merely terms of the other relating relation that relates into a complex. Still, even on this view, it is a unique feature of relations that they can fill *both* of these roles, which is what distinguishes them from just particulars that can only be terms. Now, I don't want to suggest that such multiple-role characterizations are optimal. In fact, Russell faced objections to this characterization of relations and found it difficult to explain what spurred the exhibition of such different roles within relations, as he

[13] For instance, Frank Ramsey (1925) famously argued against a number of different ways of drawing up the particular–universal distinction; in recent literature, this challenge has been elaborated upon and amplified by Fraser MacBride (2005).

understood them. But it does seem as if it is possible to assign to the same entity multiple ontological roles, although not opposing roles at the same time.

Once the ontological role(s) are specified, philosophers can start testing the adequacy of the different candidate entities for the assigned roles. If the ontological role to be played is a property role, then we might have different candidates such as classes of *possibilia*, universals, tropes, and so on. If the role is "ontological ground of distinctness of entities," possible role-fillers might be: bare particulars, substrata, states of affairs, tropes, ordinary particulars, and so forth. One might wonder if very different entities might end up playing the same ontological roles equally well, thus giving rise to equally good but incompatible rival ontological systems.

Armstrong and Lewis were remarkably intellectually honest in their debate about fundamental ontology. Given the balance of trade-offs among different theories of properties, for instance, they didn't always think that there was a straightforward winner among them. Armstrong frequently talked about how such matters could be decided "in the end game"; that is, which theory will be deemed a better one would have more to do with its overall explanatory power in a number of fields of metaphysics, and not just in the debate about properties.

I believe that this seems right. Given the unlikely situation in which two rival ontologies explain a certain phenomenon or address a certain metaphysical problem equally well, there is certainly more work to focus on in other areas of metaphysics. This is why the debate between nominalism, realism, and trope theory doesn't just end with the account of properties and relations; it also has to do with accounts one might offer, by appeal to these entities, of modality, laws of nature, propositions (if there are such), and so on. Systematic metaphysics is a difficult, gradual, and patient endeavor; it takes a great deal of thought to develop an ontology that can be employed in various areas of philosophy, and that can be used to address a number of philosophical problems.

This last point brings us back to the initial considerations of this section: namely, the importance of making sure that metaphysical problems are properly motivated and clearly stated. For if we don't have a certain amount of philosophical consensus on what the main problems are that need to be addressed, it is difficult to have agreement on which ontological roles need to be filled, since it is the problems that determine the ontological roles and the ontological roles that determine the possible categories. Absent agreement on the problems, and absent some form of general agreement on the methods, it is very difficult to make progress in ontological system-building and the evaluation of rival ontologies.

3.2.6 Some Other Ways of Approaching Ontological Categories

My preferred way of approaching ontological categories in this Element has been by appeal to ontological roles that different kinds of entities play in solving certain metaphysical problems. I believe that this bottom-up approach highlights the tight connection that exists between first-order ontological inquiry and second-order methodological inquiry. The move from the first-order domain to the meta-domain is thus not an inadvertent confusion; rather, it is in itself a methodological choice to anchor the meta-debate about categories to concrete examples and explicit goals of philosophical problem-solving.

Grossman seemed to have something similar in mind. In his *The Categorial Structure of the World*, he states that the task of ontology is to try to answer the following two questions: (1) What are the categories of the world?; and (2) What are the laws that govern these categories? (Grossman 1983, p. 3). This is not too dissimilar from the goal of chemistry, he says, with its search for the fundamental chemical elements and the laws they obey. At the same time, Grossman notes that ontology is not a science among other sciences; it has a larger scope. One starts to do ontology, he says, when one realizes not just "that there are not only different kinds of individual thing, but also different kinds of entity" (Grossman 1983, p. 3). In *The Categorial Structure of the World*, Grossman painstakingly elaborates on different categories – individuals, properties, relations, classes, structures, multitudes, and so on. But when faced with the question "what is a category?" he only says this:

> It is a kind of entity. What kind of kind? In answer to this question, we can only give examples. It is that sort of kind, as we have seen, that distinguishes between individuals, on the one hand, and properties on the other. It is that sort of kind . . . which obeys a certain kind of law, namely, categorial laws. But this reply does not really help much either. We must therefore rest content, as on so many other occasions, with examples rather than definitions. In these most fundamental matters of metaphysics, definitions are impossible. (Grossman 1983, p. 5).

Simply put, categories are *kinds* of entities, not entities themselves. Which kinds of entity? This depends on the ontology we develop. No general theory of kinds of entities is to be had, according to Grossman. In fact, he believes that "disputes about the true nature of ontology, just like similar disputes about philosophy as a whole, are singularly barren and tedious. The proof of the pudding, as the saying goes, is in the eating" (Grossman 1983, p. 18).

Some philosophers strongly disagree with this bottom-up approach to ontological categories. What motivates a top-down approach is pretty straightforward. If we take the main job of ontology to be to determine the correct list of ontological categories, then it seems central to this task to first articulate what it is we are looking for – that is, what ontological categories *are* in the first place. Take, for instance, Westerhoff's (2005) exploration of the issue. Right at the outset he finds it important to keep ontological questions separate from meta-ontological ones. The two central meta-ontological questions, according to Westerhoff, are: "1. What kind of things are ontological categories? What makes the categories incorporated in the seven systems discussed *ontological* categories?" and "2. How can these categories be related?" (Westerhoff 2005, p. 20). For him, these two questions need to be distinguished from object-level ontological questions: "1'. Which ontological categories should appear in an ontological theory?" and "2'. How are these categories in fact related, i.e. which are included in one another, which are coextensional etc.?" (Westerhoff 2005, p. 20).

Whereas Westerhoff is right that the two sets of questions are distinct, it doesn't seem to follow from this that the considerations involved in the second set should have little or no bearing on the first. Indeed, I take it that the most relevant meta-ontological questions are brought about by the first-order questions, and how one goes about answering the former will be very much influenced by how one goes about answering the latter.

A philosopher can choose to stay at a meta-ontological level, list different category systems provided by different philosophers, and then proceed to ask, following Westerhoff: What, if anything, do all these category systems, articulated by different philosophers, have in common? What are all these philosophers engaged in, when they offer a list of categories? Take, for example, Aristotle's list of categories, mentioned in Section 1.1, which appeals to substance, quantity, quality, relation, place, date, posture, state, action, and passion; Grossman's (1983) categories of simple entities (individuals, numbers, properties, relations) and complex entities (sets, structures, facts); Lowe's (2006) categories of particulars (objects, modes) and universals (kinds, attributes); Chisholm's (1996) categories of contingent entities (individuals, states) and necessary entities (states, nonstates); and so on. To ask "what makes different categories in these systems *ontological* categories?" risks, I worry, being a pseudo-question. To ask about the commonalities between different category systems assumes, without demonstrating, that there are indeed such commonalities, and that an appeal to them can explain what makes something an *ontological* category.

But the trouble here is that different philosophers often mean very different things by each of the listed categories, and the lists themselves can serve very different categorizing purposes. Now, even if we found that there are in fact certain commonalities between the distinct category systems proposed – say, their appeal to particulars, properties, relations, and so on – this *by itself* does not establish any deep meta-ontological fact. The commonalities might only be apparent – philosophers might use the same terms but articulate what they mean by them in very different ways – or they might mean similar things by their use of the term "ontological category" as well as what they mean by invoking their preferred categories such as "particulars," "universals," "relations," and so on, but what such common usage demonstrates will itself be up for interpretation and discussion. An apparent commonality in the use of terms might be due to similar patterns of thinking about categories, or it might be due to shared understanding of the implicit application conditions of the terms. In other words, it seems to me that without engaging with bottom-level ontological inquiries that undergird the introduction of these particular categories rather than some other ones, the meta-inquiry can at most provide us with a descriptivist account of what the term "ontological category" has come to mean in certain philosophical contexts.

In contrast with a descriptivist approach, the prescriptivist top-down project tries to determine what metaphysicians "ought" to mean by an "ontological category." I take this to be a more promising approach and it is one that McDaniel (2017) is favorable to in his recent work *The Fragmentation of Being*, where he argues that ontological categories should be seen as *ways of being*. He finds this approach present already in Aristotle and Aquinas, though the reference to them does not exactly help clarify the ambiguities inherent in the phrase "way of being."

It seems to me that one way of understanding the phrase is "a way of *existence*." This then leaves the door open for the view that various things can be ascribed different types of existence, and perhaps even different degrees of existence – for example, one might think that an abstract object such as a number has a different degree of existence than a concrete object such as a chair. This reading faces familiar difficulties of ontological overpopulation raised by treating existence as a predicate or a property. Another way of understanding the phrase "way of being" is as referring to one and only one being, a monistic whole of some sort, and then to think of this whole as the British idealists did, as appearing to us under different guises. Another way still is to just think of the phrase as a thinly veiled reference to most general properties, the highest determinable properties – properties, particulars, abstracta, and so on. Or, perhaps all that McDaniel has in mind is that there are some *essential properties* that determine a *kind* that ontological entities belong to, and that these *kinds* are the highest ontological categories. He writes:

> The view defended here respects the intuition that the fact that an object belongs to a particular ontological category is a deeper fact than any fact concerning the properties had by the object. The category that an object

> belongs to is not just another property among many had by the object, but rather is ontologically prior to any property had by the object. Properties partition the beings in the world. Ontological categories partition *being itself.* (McDaniel 2017, p. 124)

The language of partitioning *being itself* is not particularly helpful. But, setting that aside, McDaniel's broader intent is certainly to allow for different ontologies to fill out the details as they see fit. Some ontologies might be very coarse-grained in their appeal to only one category of entity (be it an individual or a trope), others might be very fine-grained (with many categorical subdivisions), and then there is everything else in between. This view also leaves open how one might analyze properties themselves (by appeal to natural classes, tropes, or universals).

In E. J. Lowe's (2006) *The Four Category Ontology* we find a more robust prescriptivist top-down approach to categories. Lowe describes ontology as being concerned, at its heart, with "what kinds of things can exist and co-exist" (Lowe 2006, p. 5). He immediately clarifies that by "kinds of things" he means *categories*, and that by "things" he means *entities*. Central to this project is thus determining which categories should be admitted and how they should be individuated, that is, identified and distinguished from other categories. Such categories are organized hierarchically – at the very top is the category of "entity" and right beneath it are *particulars* and *universals*, according to Lowe. The most fundamental level, however, is the third level, at which we find Lowe's four categories: kinds, properties (and relations), objects, and modes. He then goes on to define each of the four categories by appeal to two formal relations of characterization and instantiation. These relations are "formal" in the sense that, for Lowe, they are not genuine external relations and thus do not themselves fall into one of the categories; they are not themselves *entities*, though they do help explain how entities depend on one another. They are akin to *internal relations*, understood as capturing a stronger type of dependence than is usually found in internal relations.[14] Lowe grants a similar status to categories themselves. He explores whether categories could somehow fit into his system – as perhaps *kinds* or *particulars* – and quickly concludes that, given how each of his categories is defined, *category* itself is just not an entity that belongs in either of his fundamental categories. He concludes this discussion as follows: "[T]he only acceptable thing to say . . . is that the ontological

[14] Internal relations such as *taller than* supervene on the natures of the relata, in this case height. Lowe's formal relations capture internal dependence relationships which are much stronger. The example he gives is of Fido and doghood: Fido could not have existed in the absence of doghood – the two are "made for each other," so to speak (Lowe 2006, pp. 46–47).

categories are not themselves entities and are thus not to be included in an exhaustive inventory of what there is. There are, quite literally, no such things as ontological categories" (Lowe 2006, p. 43).

This fact should not, however, be taken to threaten metaphysical realism in any way. Lowe explains:

> Does this mean that no ontological system can have a realist foundation? Does it mean that ontological categorization is all just a matter of how we choose to classify and describe things – of how we choose to "carve up" reality, to use the rebarbative metaphor so often favored by anti-realists? Not at all. The difference between, say, an object and a property, or between an object and a mode, is as fundamental, objective and real as any difference could possibly be. (Lowe 2006, p. 43)

In other words, categories need not be *entities* for us to be realist about them. What they capture are real distinctions between types of entities – such as Armstrong's particulars and universals, or Lowe's modes and objects – and such distinctions are due to the *intrinsic natures* of such entities; they are not due to us and our ways of describing them. To categorize correctly is simply to categorize according to the existence and identity conditions of things that are before us. This exercise is done purely on a priori grounds, which makes it very different from the taxonomies we find in sciences such as biology or chemistry, Lowe notes.

Thus, for Lowe, ontology is a science of the most general and abstract kind – it is a science of being. In doing ontology, we are trying to discover correct ontological categories which are based on the metaphysical *natures* of entities.

> Why do we need a "science of being", and how is such a science possible? Why cannot each special science, be it empirical or *a priori*, address its own ontological questions on its own behalf, without recourse to any overarching "science of being"? The short answer to this question is that reality is one and truth indivisible. Each special science aims at truth, seeking to portray accurately some part of reality. But the various portrayals of different parts of reality must, if they are all to be true, fit together to make a portrait which can be true of reality as a whole. No special science can arrogate to itself the task of rendering mutually consistent the various partial portraits: the task can alone belong to one overarching science of being, that is, to ontology. (Lowe 2006, p. 4)

This passage captures nicely the traditional realist approach to ontology, with its bold overarching goal of discovering the most general mind-independent categories of being. This approach is an admirable and inspiring one; but, as I will argue in Section 4, it can seem alienating to anti-realists, on the one hand,

and prohibiting to more modest, revisionary, and piecemeal approaches to ontological categories, on the other.

4 On the Value of Exploring New Types of Ontological Categories

This section is more speculative and tentative in spirit. It takes a look at ways in which philosophers might break with tradition and explore new ontological categories. I start by examining one common way that the discussion between an ontological realist and an ontological anti-realist about categories plays out, and I point out aspects of the dialectical exchange that I find wanting. The anti-realist attacks tend to trivialize and misrepresent the endeavor that ontological realists are engaged in, while realists often end up alienating the more scientifically minded philosophers with their insistence that they are describing ultimate, immutable, and metaphysically necessary features of reality. I suggest a more modest, cautious, revisionary form of realism which might accommodate some of the anti-realist's concerns, without giving up on the metaphysical realist's overarching goals. I discuss the importance of trying to break out of "traditional" systems of categories and explore "new" categories.

4.1 Realism versus Anti-Realism about Ontology and Its Categories

The prevalent assumption when philosophers are devising systems of ontological categories is that they are getting at "reality as it truly is." The kinds of entities that exist and their features are assumed to be independent of us; if we succeed in reasoning well about reality and its categories, we are *discovering* the true features of mind-independent reality. This, in a nutshell, is realism. Anti-realism disagrees; it claims that the ontological categories that philosophers come up with are not getting at mind-independent reality, but are rather describing our own conceptual apparatus. According to anti-realists, it's not the case that there *is* a mind-independent reality, but that we cannot properly get at it; this would still be a form of realism, just a pessimistic kind. For anti-realists, there simply is no mind-independent system of categories to be had.

We can more easily see how one might be an anti-realist about aesthetic qualities such as beauty – these are often taken to lie in the eye of the beholder; but it might seem more difficult to argue for anti-realism about things such as planets, dogs, trees, water molecules, and such. The latter do not appear to depend upon a judging mind for their existence. Anti-realists can counter such observations in a couple of ways: one is to argue that genuine agreement on the things that realists assume must be uncontroversial does not exist (simply, there are no clear-cut cases to be had; dogs, trees, and planets are no different than mind-dependent qualities such as color or taste). Another way for an anti-realist to proceed is to accept that there are genuine commonalities among people's judgments, but argue that this form of agreement is merely a contingent feature of human perception, cognition, and psychology.

It is not my aim here to engage in depth with the different types and facets of the realist–anti-realist debate as it applies to ontology. What I do want to bring out, however, are the different values that a realist and an anti-realist end up placing on ontological categories and ontological commitments. It is not uncommon to hear realists worry that ontology, and metaphysics more broadly, would lose its value within an anti-realist framework. "If we were merely engaged in describing how the world appears to us, and if we were merely describing our own conceptual schemas, then ontology would no longer be a study of the most fundamental categories of being and it would lose its value," the realist's reasoning goes. "This is why we are engaged in finding out the *truth* about how reality is. We are after the godly perspective, the *sub specie aeternitatis* view of reality," they add. Anti-realists, however, often seem completely unfazed by this: "In that case, so much worse for ontology," they say. Realists' insistence on devising ontological categories strikes them as an idle endeavor, with no real consequences for anyone except those interested in a very narrow metaphysical debate. This is, of course, a bit of a caricature, but it does illustrate well what is at stake. Now let's look at a concrete example.

In their recent article, Bueno et al. (2015) advocate for an ontology without categories; in doing so, the authors reenact a version of the exchange just described. They specifically take aim at Lowe's (2006) four-category ontology and his arguments for the realist stance about ontological categories. The authors highlight Lowe's repeated appeal to indispensability arguments for the categories that he proposes:

> The indispensability argument is central to Jonathan Lowe's general defense of the fairly traditional project of metaphysics, but also to his articulation of the need for a metaphysical type of possibility and for the grounds for embracing distinctively metaphysical objects of the sorts covered by his four primary ontological categories: kinds, attributes, modes, and objects. Each plays a metaphysical role that it and only it can play, not only within the philosopher's domain of metaphysics, but also in the various domains of the specialized sciences which, according to him, could not be as they are, were there none of the objects with which he populates his four-category ontology. (Bueno et al. 2015, pp. 234–235)

Bueno et al. (2015) find such pervasive appeal to indispensability unconvincing. They don't much engage with the specifics of the case that Lowe makes for the introduction of each of the categories; their main focus is on Lowe's claim that his proposed categories are indispensable for scientific enterprise. For example, Lowe criticizes regularity accounts of laws of nature as unsatisfactory and believes that conceiving of laws of nature in terms of relations between universals provides a better foundation for their generality and predictive power. The authors reply to this is that Lowe's proposal is "unlikely to be recognizable to practitioners of science as a proper solution to the problem" (Bueno et al. 2015, p. 242). Lowe also believes that his ontological categories are routinely presupposed by scientific descriptions of the world, as these make pervasive appeals to kinds, objects, properties, and so on. But the authors find this claim to be extremely problematic. They say that Lowe's categories are indeed dispensable, since they are of no concern to a practicing scientist.

I find that there is something strange about these arguments. It is as if Bueno et al. (2015) are purposely missing the point that a realist is trying to make: namely, Lowe is not claiming that all scientists need to do metaphysics first, by reading, for instance, his account of ontological categories as a prerequisite for their scientific research. Nor is he claiming that all scientists need to learn about universals and his own account of laws of nature. The uncharitableness of interpretation that anti-realists are engaged in is striking. What Lowe *is* claiming, however, is that scientific reasoning presupposes the very categories that he has outlined; he claims that if scientists were to ask themselves foundational questions about features of laws of nature, they could use some metaphysical background on universals. The types of criticism of ontological realism that appeal to what scientists do in their practice are thus entirely beside the point.

Perhaps the upshot of these anti-realist arguments is just that Lowe, and realist approaches to ontology more generally, are overplaying their hand. There are no genuinely indispensable categories, claim anti-realists. We need categor*izations*, since we need to sort and categorize things, but we should not assume – the claim goes – that the entities subsumed under such categorizations pick out mind-independent entities. "Categorizations without reification" is their motto; Bueno et al. (2015) believe that abstract concepts rather than categories can do the categorizing job well enough. Concepts are flexible, easily swapped around, eliminated, and introduced as needed. Categories, in contrast, are not so flexible, according to Bueno et al.; they seem rigid and permanent.

Now, what should be noted is that these anti-realist concerns seem to rely on a particular understanding of the nature of truth, which is antithetical to the realist conception. The backdrop to the realist's commitment to ontological categories is some form of correspondence theory of truth. In truthmaker terms, the assumption can be put simply as follows: there are truthbearers, assertions that are either true or false, and truthmakers, worldly facts or states of affairs that make those sentences true. For example, "this piece of paper is white" is made true by the way things are, in this case, by this piece of paper indeed being white. Whereas we can express the meaning of a given sentence in different ways, truthmakers are what they are, they exist independently of our minds, as does the truthmaking relationship between truthbearers and the facts that make them true. One can provide different ontological accounts of truthmakers (nominalists might appeal to particulars and their class membership; trope theorists will appeal to tropes and trope-bundles; immanent realists will appeal to particulars, universals, and possibly states of affairs), but the assumption is that there are some such entities. One can also take different attitudes toward the scope of the truthmaker approach –that is, whether one ought to be a truthmaker maximalist and take it that *all* truths must have truthmakers, or argue more modestly that perhaps some truths, such as negative truths or general truths, do not have a truthmaker – but the assumption is nonetheless that truthmaking applies widely.

In any case, anti-realists must reject all of this. They must reject correspondence and assume some other theory of truth – perhaps a coherence theory, or the pragmatist theory, or the deflationary theory. But such theories are notoriously incapable of *explaining* what it is that makes sentences true and what might guide one in evaluating the truth of a given sentence. Such theories are also quite incapable of explaining what it is that makes certain concepts better than others for categorizing purposes. If a certain concept is more useful, or serves a certain purpose better than other concepts, how should such usage or purpose be characterized and what makes one concept better than another? Why apply the concept "rectangularity" to all of the things we perceive to be rectangular? Or what do all of our appeals to "objects" have in common? If there is no appeal to what the concepts pick out, and no specified criteria of applicability of concepts, then it becomes very difficult to have a meaningful conversation with an anti-realist. If, on the other hand, anti-realists have already tacitly assumed that certain concepts are better than others because they pick out certain features of reality better than others, then they seem to have relied upon some form of correspondence theory after all. In that case, the dispute with the realist is no longer about whether or not we ought to admit ontological categories, but rather about *which* ontological categories should be admitted.

Thus, rather than locate their disagreement at the general level of concepts versus categories, many anti-realists might actually just be disagreeing about particular types of reifications – they might not believe in universals and might find the entire debate about their features, multiple occurrences, instantiations, and so forth pointless and off-putting. Similarly with relations, and perhaps some other types of ontological postulates. Or, maybe they simply do not believe in the existence of the most general determinables – such as being a property, being a relation, being an object, being a kind, being an abstract entity, being a concrete entity, and so on. But this too is an intratheoretical dispute about *which* ontological categories should be admitted, not *whether* they should be admitted. Indeed, whenever these theorists appeal to certain objects rather than others, whenever they describe properties of these objects and expect to be understood and agreed or disagreed with, their talk of mind-dependent concepts ends up looking like a thinly veiled implicit commitment to certain fundamental ontological categories.

Thus, although anti-realists might find it quite tempting to eliminate reference to ontological categories altogether, it might be wiser to proceed with caution. A revisionist approach might be a better way forward than wholesale elimination. For, as I have tried to show, it is often not clear how deep the disagreement between the two sides actually goes, especially in light of the fact that concept-talk often ends up actually presupposing at least some of the categories it is trying to rid itself of.

4.2 Benefits of the Ontological-Role Approach to Categories

Another factor that drives the anti-realist pushback of the kind described by Bueno et al. (2015) has to do with the perceived rigidity, inflexibility, and absoluteness of categories. Recall how Lowe, in the quote at the end of Section 3.2.6, answers the following two questions: “Why do we need a ‘science of being’, and how is such a science possible? Why cannot each special science, be it empirical or *a priori*, address its own ontological questions on its own behalf, without recourse to any overarching ‘science of being’?” (Lowe 2006, p. 4). He says that “reality is one and truth indivisible” and that whereas “special sciences” aim to portray some part of reality correctly, these different portrayals must all fit together to make an accurate picture of reality as a whole. It is thus the job of ontology, according to Lowe, to paint this accurate picture of such a holistic reality.

I suspect that this underlying commitment to oneness of reality and the supposed indivisibility of truth alienates some scientifically minded philosophers. The appeal to this oneness can appear to leave no room for partial explorations and piecemeal pursuits of truth to count as fully fledged truths in their own right. *If* all of these different partial explorations must add up to *one* reality described properly only by the *one* correct ontology in order to count as descriptions of reality, and *if* various truths must all add up to *one indivisible truth*, then only those engaged in the “science of everything” will stand a chance of getting at *the truth*. And that seems like a tall order indeed.

I am not sure, however, that Lowe intended to embrace this sort of monistic picture, despite sometimes sounding as if he did. For instance, he writes:

> The relativist must hold that reality itself is many, not one – that we do not all inhabit the same world. He must say that the sum total of existence for me is not necessarily the same as the sum total of existence for you. ... Against [pluralist ontologies] is posed a monistic ontology which holds that reality is fundamentally one: that there is just one sum total of existence – one world – which is the same for all thinkers, places and times. And my suggestion is that, to the extent that we are committed to the unity of truth, at least inasmuch as this amounts to an unconditional acceptance of the principle of non-contradiction, we are committed to the oneness of reality and to its mind-independence. We are committed, in short, to a fully realist metaphysics. Fortunately, this still leaves plenty of scope for many forms of pluralism. In accepting that reality is one, we need not accept that there is only one truth, or only one truthmaker, or only one kind of truthmaker. Our ontology will admit of multitudes within The One. (Lowe 2006, p. 191)

In this passage we can see that what drives Lowe to think in apparent monistic terms about reality is the concern about truth. The unity or indivisibility of truth mentioned here simply has to do with what he calls "an unconditional acceptance of the principle of non-contradiction." There cannot be a truth according to you and a truth according to me, for this would inevitably lead to a reality of contradictions, and this simply cannot be, for Lowe. For there to be no violation of the principle of non-contradiction, the truth must be mind-independent and the reality that our true descriptions attempt to get at, must be *one*. It is *one* not in the almost mystical sense of the British idealists; rather, it is *one* in the sense that it is a *shared reality*.

Seen in this way, ambitious metaphysical realist projects like Lowe's in fact leave plenty of room for scientific and metaphysical explorations of all kinds. They leave room for the metaphysical problem-driven, bottom-up approach to ontology that I favor, as well.

Admittedly, the piecemeal approach is less ambitious, but in spite of it (or because of it), it might just be more fruitful. In Section 3, I suggested that approaching the search for fundamental ontological categories is best done within the framework of ontological roles. Metaphysical problems determine the ontological roles that need to be played (such as property roles, particular roles, relation roles, etc.) and the roles, in turn, characterize the sorts of entities – ontological categories – that can fill them (universals for both property and relation roles, states of affair or trope-bundles for roles of particulars, etc.).

The hope is that such a framing of the issues will highlight the fact that determining the categories of entities is not done outside of a specific problem-solving context. It allows for a more transparent debate about the ways that metaphysical problems get stated; it stresses the importance of guarding against engaging in pseudo-problems; and it helps us set up criteria of comparison between different candidate entities and systems.

Saying that ontological roles characterize ontological categories does not mean that *all* ontological roles need to be filled by a category of entity. Ontological roles that need to be filled can be large and small, and some such roles might need to be filled by entities, while others might be filled with conceptual distinctions. Thus, whereas categories should be characterized by appeal to ontological roles, not all roles need to be played by categories.

Ontological categories need not merely be of the highest level. It seems wise to leave it open how fine-grained one might like the ontological categories to be. As I noted in Section 3, the highest determinables for a realist about universals will not themselves be universals, but the lowest, most specific determinates certainly will be. Will the lowest determinates such as *being crimson* or *being rectangular* themselves be categories? I believe that it will depend on the explanatory roles assigned to them, within a given theory. Although the highest categories will likely be set in stone within a particular theory, the lower categories might not be set at all; and that is a good thing, for it allows for all kinds of revisionary projects within metaphysical systems.

I will here illustrate just two such cases of category revisions. The first example comes to us from A. N. Whitehead (1920), with his ontology of events as the highest category of entity. The second example comes from a relatively recent reframing of gender categories.

4.2.1 Whitehead's Temporal Ontology of Events

In various category systems, one usually finds place and time listed as the highest categories that cut across those of, say, facts, or particulars, or properties. But A.N. Whitehead (1920) offered a radically new and interesting temporal ontology that made no such separation. He explicitly argued against what he called "a bifurcation of nature" into two systems of reality. One reality was the given physical reality, say, the reality of microphysics with entities such as electrons, protons, and other microparticles; the other reality he referred to was the mind-dependent one, or what is given to us in our sense-awareness. What Whitehead was getting at is, essentially, the distinction between Lockean primary and secondary qualities, a distinction that he took to be wrong and pernicious. The so-called bifurcation of nature, according to Whitehead, created a schism that induced us to arrive at wrong conclusions about both realms. The way forward, then, was to close the schism, by assuming that "everything perceived is in nature. We may not pick and choose. For us the red glow of the sunset should be as much part of nature as are the molecules and electric waves by which men of science would explain the phenomenon. It is for natural philosophy to analyze how these various elements of nature are connected"

(Whitehead 1920, p. 29). Whitehead's way of closing the gap between the two realms was thus not to pick one realm over the other, but rather, to integrate them.

The result of this approach was a highly original temporal ontology, with irreducibly dynamic events and processes at its core. Whitehead (1920) conceived of events as chunks of passage of nature, and thought of objects as what remains the same through time, through all the change and flux. Objects, for him, are always to be found within events, and could only be isolated through the process of abstraction. The traditional particular–universal distinction was scrapped and replaced by an event–object distinction in Whitehead's temporal ontology.

As we saw in Section 2, the particular–universal distinction emerged from the recognition of genuine resemblance in the world, and from the need to explain and ontologically ground this phenomenon in some way. Universals were introduced as entities that ground such resemblances by being present in each particular that has an apparent property. Particulars, in this framework, provided the ground of distinctness of entities. In such a context, change was often seen as a state of dissimilarity, described in static terms such as: a particular, a, has a certain property, F, at a certain time, t_1, and then a different property, G, at time t_2. But Whitehead's event–object distinction turned this picture on its head. The background assumption in his ontology is the constant change and transitoriness in nature. Nature appears to us as passing and changing, and events are the basic currency of that temporal passage. Objects are then derived as what *seems to us* to be constant in that change; what we can grasp and abstract from it.

Interestingly, what helped lead Whitehead to this change in perspective was the idea of seeing ourselves and our perceptions of reality as an integral part of it: "sense-awareness and thought are themselves processes"; in addition to what ordinarily gets considered as passage in nature, we need to consider that "there is a passage of sense-awareness and a passage of thought" (Whitehead 1920, p. 66). He even adds: "We may speculate, if we like, that this alliance of the passage of mind with the passage of nature arises from their both sharing in some ultimate character of passage which dominates all being" (Whitehead 1920, p. 69). It is a matter for a different investigation to consider how successful Whitehead's unified approach to ontology really is. Here, I just wanted to point out that there is merit in exploring attempts similar to his, as they reveal different ontological categorizations that are worth taking seriously.

In their piece on blind spots in physics and scientific inquiry more broadly, physicists Frank and Gleiser, and philosopher Thompson (Frank et al. 2019), apply Whitehead's insight to the study of time and the study of consciousness.

They argue that we mustn't lose sight of how experientially charged the objects of scientific inquiry really are; overlooking this fact leads to an unwarranted faith in science as providing absolute knowledge:

> When we look at the objects of scientific knowledge, we don't tend to see the experiences that underpin them. We do not see how experience makes their presence to us possible. Because we lose sight of the necessity of experience, we erect a false idol of science as something that bestows absolute knowledge of reality, independent of how it shows up and how we interact with it. (Frank et al. 2019)

This belief in absolute knowledge leads to blind spots: "The Blind Spot arises when we start to believe that this [scientific] method gives us access to unvarnished reality. But experience is present at every step. Scientific models must be pulled out from observations, often mediated by our complex scientific equipment. They are idealizations, not actual things in the world" (Frank et al. 2019). They conclude: "[T]o finally 'see' the Blind Spot is to wake up from a delusion of absolute knowledge. It's also to embrace the hope that we can create a new scientific culture, in which we see ourselves both as an expression of nature and as a source of nature's self-understanding" (Frank et al. 2019).

All this is very broad and it is not entirely clear how such an insight is to be applied on a case-by-case basis. Nonetheless, there is something valuable here that we can apply to metaphysical investigations as well as the scientific ones. It does seem to be the case that certain blind spots in metaphysics arise in a similar way to the ones described – that is, they arise when we start to take our *models* of reality, our rough generalizations and categorizations, for the reality itself. Whitehead was particularly worried about this when discussing the notion of an instant of time, a construct he took to be useful but ultimately very misleading when it comes to the true nature of physical reality. He puts this concern as follows:

> Instantaneousness is the concept of all nature at an instant, where an instant is conceived as deprived of all temporal extension. For example we conceive of the distribution of matter in space at an instant. This is a very useful concept in science especially in applied mathematics; but it is a very complex idea so far as concerns its connexions with the immediate facts of sense-awareness. *There is no such thing as nature at an instant posited by sense-awareness. What sense-awareness delivers over for knowledge is nature through a period.* (Whitehead 1920, p. 57, italics mine).

This passage nicely illustrates Whitehead's motivation for disposing of instants as genuine features of physical reality. For him, we need to begin our study of nature from our experience of it, and what experience offers are only temporally extended events, not instantaneous entities. Instants, he says at one point, are "a metaphysical fairytale." This does not mean, though, that we are to dispose of instants altogether. Just because instants are not given in our sense-awareness does not mean that they are not useful abstractions in mathematics and science. What we must not lose track of is that they are just that – useful abstractions. And, for Whitehead, abstractions should not be substituted for reality, which they are introduced to describe and explain,. Thus, we should take Whitehead seriously when he warns: "[W]e are apt to fall into the error of thinking that the facts are simple because simplicity is the goal of our quest. The guiding motto in the life of every natural philosopher should be 'Seek simplicity and distrust it'." (Whitehead 1920, p. 163).

Even if one disagrees with the particulars of Whitehead's ontological proposal, the motto he offers is instructive. The change of perspective that his denial of the bifurcation of nature offers is illuminating. By integrating our experience of change with the passage of nature itself, he fused the two sets of categories that are often kept separate – space and time, on the one hand, and atemporal categories such as particulars and universals, on the other. The result is surprising and makes us reconsider whether passage and change should indeed be derived from a static picture of reality, or whether passage and flux of nature should come first with static entities derived as abstractions from it.

4.2.2 Reframing of Gender Categories

In social ontology, discussions of ontological categories are particularly consequential for our practical concerns. Take, for instance, the question of whether *gender* is a genuine mid-range ontological category, and whether it should be used to categorize people into only two distinct groups of *men* and *women*. Many have thought that how one answers this metaphysical question ought to guide one's use of gender terms, but Barnes (2020) has recently argued against this straightforward alignment.

Indeed, "in virtue of what, if anything, do people have genders?" seems to be a distinctly metaphysical question. In her recent paper Barnes (2020) nicely summarizes two broad types of answers that this question has received in recent literature: (1) social-position accounts, which explain gender by appeal to external factors; and (2) identity-based accounts, which explain gender by appeal to internal factors.

Social-position accounts tend to explain gender by appeal to external social factors such as how people are perceived, or what social roles they are expected to play in society, and so on. For Witt (2011), for example, gender seems to play a pretty fundamental role in structuring and ordering other social properties and roles. She takes human beings to be comprised of *the human organism*, *the person*, and *the social individual*. Gender is then a social property that structures and unifies other social roles which come to be part of the social individual. For example, I am not just a parent, I am a mother; I am not just a spouse, I am a wife; I am not just a sibling, I am a sister; and so on. Gender thus has a central social role that is imposed on persons based on various assumptions about the reproductive role that they play. Haslanger (2012), too, is a proponent of the social-position account of gender, but in her definitions of women and men, she makes salient the structural features of society which consistently place women in subordinate roles and positions based on their perceived or imagined bodily features, and which place men in privileged roles and positions based on their perceived or imagined bodily features.

Barnes notes that the trouble with social-position accounts is that they face what Jenkins (2016) has called an “exclusion problem.” That is, such accounts tend to leave out of their classifications trans women and trans men if they are not perceived by others as falling into these social categories. By relying merely on how others in society perceive and engage with a person, and not on how people themselves identify, social-position accounts fail to capture an important aspect of gender – the relevant first-person reports of people themselves.

Identity-based accounts avoid the exclusion problem just described by putting weight, in their explanations of gender, on the *internal* features of persons. What matters is how one feels about oneself, how one identifies, which groups one sees oneself as belonging to, and so on. This kind of view is endorsed by McKitrick (2015) in her appeal to behavioral dispositions. If a person has a certain number of dispositions identified as feminine (such as how they tend to express themselves in various contexts, how they dress, how they wear their hair and makeup, what name they go by, which bathroom they choose, and so on), then that person is a woman. But the trouble with these kinds of accounts is that though they avoid the previous exclusion problem, they face a problem of their own. The worry here is that if too much weight is put on a person’s own self-identification and expression of gender, it might leave out those who are not actively engaged, or not *able* to engage in this kind of self-sorting activity. The example that Barnes (2020) discusses here is of cognitively disabled women and men who, it seems, should not be excluded from being identified as women or men just because they lack the capacities for explicit self-identification.

Barnes herself ends up endorsing a modified social-position account of gender. She finds this account to be important insofar as it tracks social reality well. At the same time, she admits that such an account far from offers a complete story; gender, according to her, also encompasses gender identity, gender expression, and so on. In the light of the discussion of the messiness and difficulties in characterizing gender categories, Barnes insists that gender terms should not be expected to neatly track such categories. She makes a strong case for keeping the application of gender terms as permissive and flexible as possible, while at the same time recognizing the social reality captured by the social-position accounts. In this way, the flexible use of these terms is meant to help the process of overcoming the still very real and grim social reality of gender inequality.

These sorts of discussions are clearly important and relevant although they do not engage with traditional metaphysics of the highest ontological categories of substance, mode, and property. But exploring the status of mid- to lower-level categories such as gender or race is important and revealing. We find important truths when we ask whether such categories are genuine; in what way they should be defined; what role they play in current social and political reality; and whether or not we should worry if our terms pick these categories neatly or not. These are all questions that a revisionist ontological project makes room for.

4.3 Concluding Remarks: Ontological Progress and the Revisionist Project

I conclude with a few words to the skeptic who, after reading my discussion of ontological categories in this Element, is left wondering whether the whole project is utterly hopeless. They might think that if, after more than two and a half millennia since Plato's discussion of Forms, philosophers have not yet even remotely settled on fundamental ontological categories, what hope can there be for progress in ontology, or metaphysics, or philosophy more broadly?

I believe that such a pessimism is too hasty and that a lot depends on how we interpret progress in philosophy. In his recent paper, Daly (2016) equates the presumed lack of progress with persistent philosophical disagreement, that is, the fact that no philosophical problem appears to have been permanently solved. He then goes on to explore three different explanations for this lack of progress: (1) Russell's explanation, which contrasts science and philosophy; (2) MacBride's explanation, which invokes "the epistemic end of days"; and (3) the explanation that appeals to the notion of cognitive closure.

Russell's explanation is succinct: he claims that science is "what you more or less know" whereas philosophy is "what you do not know," thus contrasting the presumed certainty of science with the speculative nature of philosophy. Russell also pointed out that science has been successful at solving some of the problems that initially originated as philosophical ones. But, as Daly (2016) rightly points out, this Russellian characterization of both science's certainty and philosophy's uncertainty is not accurate. There is a fair amount of speculation in science itself;

we just need to turn our attention to theoretical physics. So, Russell's account is not helpful in diagnosing the reason for the presumed lack of philosophical progress.

MacBride's (2014) explanation attributes the lack of philosophical progress to the fact that philosophical problems have a broad range – they are both general and require understanding of several areas of knowledge. So, until the supposed "epistemic end of days" we cannot expect progress to happen because of the deep interconnectedness of philosophical problems with each other, and with problems in other adjacent disciplines. Daly (2016) finds this account objectionable as well, because, according to him, it exaggerates the degree to which philosophical problems are indeed interconnected. Many problems in science are deeply interconnected too, notes Daly, but that by itself does not translate into a lack of progress.

I am particularly intrigued by the idea of the "epistemic end of days" and wonder if a similar hypothesis can help us think about progress in philosophy and the nature of our discipline more broadly. Imagine an omniscient being: Does such a being philosophize? And, more to the point, does such a being do ontology and engage in the search for ontological categories? If we are inclined to say "no, the omniscient being does not engage in ontological inquiry," such an answer would likely be based on the following thought: when one does ontology, one is engaged in the discovery of ontological facts; such facts are perhaps, as MacBride (2014) suggests, extremely difficult to get right. But a higher omniscient being would surely have no trouble grasping them. Such a being would not need to engage in philosophical pursuit any more than it would need to engage in scientific pursuits, experiments, and so on. If, however, we thought that an omniscient being would indeed do philosophy, such an answer might indicate several things. It could reveal a view of philosophy as riddled with puzzles that no amount of factual knowledge can solve; or it could reveal a view of philosophy as a process of reasoning of a particular type, with different possible outcomes, due to different possible combinations of views as well as patterns of reasoning. I am sure there are more possibilities still; the goal of the question "does an omniscient being philosophize?" is simply to help us see that the question of philosophical progress perhaps has less to do with the disagreements we have with one another and more to do with our understanding of the very nature of philosophy and philosophical pursuit.

Related to this discussion is the third explanation of the lack of philosophical progress with its appeal to our presumed cognitive closure. Daly attributes this view to Van Inwagen (2008), and the thought is simply that we cannot make progress in philosophy because our minds are cognitively closed to solutions of philosophical problems; our minds are simply not up to the task. I find this kind of explanation to be the most hopeless of all, as it amounts to suggesting that we might as well just give up – our philosophical pursuits are the vacuous exercise of an incompetent mind. It is quite ironic that such a suggestion comes from one of the most prominent contemporary metaphysicians.

This approach can be rebuffed, of course, by questioning the claim that we are cognitively closed to solutions of philosophical problems. For what is it, exactly, about our cognitive capacities that makes us particularly incapable of finding solutions to philosophical problems, but allows us to find solutions to scientific or mathematical problems? This last question shows us the way out – that is, it shows us that we have been focusing on the wrong side of the issue. Rather than worry about the presumed lack of *solutions* to philosophical problems, we should be focusing on the *formulations* of our problems.

Daly draws a similar conclusion about methodology. He believes that "the fault doesn't lie with the questions we ask – that they are somehow defective – or with our minds – that they are ill-suited or too limited – but with the methods and ambitions involved in our inquiry" (Daly 2016, pp. 35–36). Daly takes philosophical methods to be at once too weak and too strong. They are too weak, because one can always question the justification and the evidence for the premises, even in deductive arguments. And they are too strong in the sense that no conclusion is safe – it is subject to the same scrutiny that the premises of the argument are subjected to. Philosophical ambitions are also at fault, according to Daly, since philosophy "seeks to identify the most fundamental level of epistemic justification for claims, and it aspires to an especially high degree of clarity and understanding" (Daly 2016, p. 38).

I tend to agree with the spirit of Daly's diagnosis, though not with the details. First, it is not clear to me that a presumed lack of progress in philosophy should be deduced from the persistence of disagreement. Persistence of disagreement in philosophy can be seen as its feature, perhaps even a philosophical virtue, a sign of healthy skepticism within a discipline that is highly speculative but also uniquely self-reflective and self-questioning. Moreover, a case can be made that there has been a tremendous amount of progress in philosophy across the board, as well as in ontology more specifically. Often times it seems as if there are very few stones that philosophers have left unturned, very few arguments or avenues that have been left unexplored.

But there is room for improvement, of course, and I believe that philosophical methods need to be further scrutinized and better regimented. I have argued that part of this task is to engage in a more careful analysis of the formulations of the problems we set out to address, by being more transparent about the underlying motivations and implicit assumptions. I also agree with Daly's concern about philosophical ambitions, though I see the concern as having more to do with the level of generality than with the aims themselves that philosophers set their sights on.

I find that as admirable as systematic metaphysical top-down theory-building is, there should also be room for more piecemeal and humble approaches to ontology. Trying to carry out both projects is probably the best way forward, since if we only take the global approach, we might miss catching the blind spots and/or force the categorizations top-down in a way that may not fit the different philosophical phenomena in need of explanation. If, on the other hand, we only take the piecemeal approach, we might miss the ways that different areas of inquiry hang together, and miss out on the big picture that drives the commitment to the most fundamental ontological categories. The most fruitful way forward is probably the one that puts forward an initial system, but in various areas keeps amending and refining the categories, as needed.

References

Ackrill, J. L. (1963). *Aristotle: Categories and De Interpretatione*. Oxford: Clarendon Press.

Armstrong, D. M. (1978). *Nominalism and Realism: Universals and Scientific Realism*, Volume I. Cambridge: Cambridge University Press.

(1983). *What Is a Law of Nature?* New York: Columbia University Press.

(1997a). "Against 'Ostrich' Nominalism: A Reply to Michael Devitt." In D. H. Mellor and A. Oliver eds., *Properties*. Oxford: Oxford University Press, 1997, 101–111. [Original date of publication 1980.]

(1997b). *A World of States of Affairs*. Cambridge: Cambridge University Press.

Barnes, E. (2019). "Gender and Gender Terms." *Noûs*, 54/3, 704–730.

Baumer, M. (1993). "Chasing Aristotle's Categories Down the Tree of Grammar." *Journal of Philosophical Research*, 18, 341–449.

Bradley, F. H. (1893). *Appearance and Reality*. Oxford: Clarendon Press.

(1910). "On Appearance, Error and Contradiction." *Mind*, 19/74, 153–185.

(1911). "Reply to Mr. Russell's Explanations." *Mind*, 20/77, 74–76.

Bueno, O., Busch, J., and Shalkowski, S. A. (2015). "The No-Category Ontology." *The Monist*, 98/3, 233–245.

Cameron, R. P. (2008). "Turtles All the Way Down: Regress, Priority and Fundamentality." *Philosophical Quarterly*, 58/230, 1–14.

Campbell, K. (1990). *Abstract Particulars*. Oxford: Basil Blackwell.

Cargile, J. (2003). "On Russell's Argument against Resemblance Nominalism." *Australasian Journal of Philosophy*, 81/4, 549–560.

Chisholm, R. M. (1996). *A Realistic Theory of Categories: An Essay on Ontology*. Cambridge: Cambridge University Press.

Conee, E., and Sider, T. (2007). *Riddles of Existence: A Guided Tour of Metaphysics*. Oxford: Oxford University Press.

Correia, F. (2008). "Ontological Dependence." *Philosophy Compass*, 3/5, 1013–1032.

Daly, C. (2016). "Persistent Philosophical Disagreement." *Proceedings of the Aristotelian Society*, 1, 3–25.

Della Rocca, M. (2010). "PSR." *Philosopher's Imprint*, 10/7, 1–13.

Frank, A., Gleiser, M., and Thompson, E. (2019). "The Blind Spot." *Aeon*, January 8. https://aeon.co/essays/the-blind-spot-of-science-is-the-neglect-of-lived-experience.

Grossman, R. (1983). *The Categorial Structure of the World*. Bloomington: Indiana University Press.

Grünbaum, A. (2009). "Why Is There a World At All, Rather Than Just Nothing?" *Ontology Studies*, 9, 7–19.

Haslanger, S. (2012). *Resisting Reality: Social Construction and Social Critique*. New York: Oxford University Press.

Jackson, F. C. (1977). "Statements about Universals." *Mind*, 86/343, 427–429.

Jenkins, K. (2016). "Amelioration and Inclusion: Gender Identity and the Concept of Woman." *Ethics*, 126/2, 394–421.

Johnson, W. E. (1921). *Logic*. Cambridge: Cambridge University Press.

Lewis, D. (1973). "Counterfactuals and Comparative Possibility." *Journal of Philosophical Logic*, 2/4, 418–446.

(1983). "New Work for a Theory of Universals." *Australasian Journal of Philosophy*, 61, 343–377.

Lowe, E. J. (2006). *The Four-Category Ontology: A Metaphysical Foundation for Natural Science*. Oxford: Clarendon Press.

(2018). "Metaphysics as the Science of Essence." In A. Carruth, S. Gibb, and J. Heil eds., *Ontology, Modality, and Mind: Themes from the Metaphysics of E.J. Lowe.* Oxford: Oxford University Press, 14–34.

MacBride, F. (2005). "The Particular–Universal Distinction: A Dogma of Metaphysics?" *Mind*, 114, 565–614.

(2014). "Analytic Philosophy and Its Synoptic Commission: Towards the Epistemic End of Days." *Royal Institute of Philosophy Supplement*, 74, 221–236.

Maurin, A.-S. (2018). "Tropes." In Edward N. Zalta ed., *The Stanford Encyclopedia of Philosophy.* https://plato.stanford.edu/entries/tropes/.

McDaniel, K. (2017). *The Fragmentation of Being*. Oxford: Oxford University Press.

McKitrick, J. (2015). "A Dispositional Account of Gender." *Philosophical Studies*, 172/10, 2575–2589.

Nolan, D. (2001). "What's Wrong with Infinite Regresses?" *Metaphilosophy*, 32/5, 523–538.

Oliver, A. (1996). "The Metaphysics of Properties." *Mind*, 105, 1–80.

Pap, A. (1959). "Nominalism, Empiricism and Universals: I." *Philosophical Quarterly*, 9/37, 330–340.

Perović, K. (2015). "The Importance of Russell's Regress Argument for Universals." In D. Wishon and B. Linsky eds., *Acquaintance, Knowledge, and Logic: New Essays on Bertrand Russell's The Problems of Philosophy*, 171–187. Stanford, CA: CSLI Publications.

(2016). "A Neo-Armstrongian Defense of States of Affairs: A Reply to Vallicella." *Metaphysica*, 17/2, 143–161.

Plato. (1963). *The Collected Dialogues*, ed. E. Hamilton and H. Cairns. Princeton, NJ: Princeton University Press.

Quine, W. V. (1951). "Ontology and ideology." *Philosophical Studies: An International Journal for Philosophy in the Analytic Tradition*, 2/1, 11–15.

(1997). "On What There Is." In D. H. Mellor and A. Oliver eds., *Properties*. Oxford: Oxford University Press, 74–88. [Original date of publication 1948.]

Ramsey, F. P. (1925). "Universals." *Mind*, 34/136, 401–417.

Rodriguez-Pereyra, G. (2002). *Resemblance Nominalism*. Oxford: Oxford University Press.

(2004). "Paradigms and Russell's Resemblance Regress." *Australasian Journal of Philosophy*, 82/4, 644–651.

Russell, B. (1911). "On the Relations of Universals and Particulars." *Proceedings of the Aristotelian Society*, 12, 1–24.

(1912). *The Problems of Philosophy*. London: William & Norgate.

(1992). *Theory of Knowledge: The 1913 Manuscript*. New York: Routledge.

Schaffer, J. (2012). "Grounding, Transitivity, and Contrastivity." In F. Correia and B. Schneider eds., *Metaphysical Grounding: Understanding the Structure of Reality*. Cambridge: Cambridge University Press, 122–138.

Simons, P. (1994). "Particulars in Particular Clothing: Three Trope Theories of Substance." *Philosophy and Phenomenological Research*, 54/3, 553–575.

Studtmann, P. (2021). "Aristotle's Categories." In Edward N. Zalta ed., *The Stanford Encyclopedia of Philosophy*. https://plato.stanford.edu/entries/aristotle-categories/.

Tahko, T. E. (2018). "Fundamentality." In Edward N. Zalta ed., *The Stanford Encyclopedia of Philosophy*. https://plato.stanford.edu/entries/fundamentality/.

Tahko, T. E., and Lowe, E. J. (2020). "Ontological Dependence." In Edward N. Zalta ed., *The Stanford Encyclopedia of Philosophy*. https://plato.stanford.edu/entries/dependence-ontological/.

Van Inwagen, P. (2008). *Metaphysics*. 3rd ed. Boulder, Co: Westview Press.

Westerhoff, J. (2005). *Ontological Categories*. Oxford: Clarendon Press.

Whitehead, A. N. (1919). *An Enquiry concerning the Principles of Natural Knowledge*. Cambridge: Cambridge University Press.

(1920). *The Concept of Nature*. Cambridge: Cambridge University Press.

Witt, C. (2011). *The Metaphysics of Gender*. Oxford: Oxford University Press.

Cambridge Elements ☰

Metaphysics

Tuomas E. Tahko
University of Bristol

Tuomas E. Tahko is Professor of Metaphysics of Science at the University of Bristol, UK. Tahko specializes in contemporary analytic metaphysics, with an emphasis on methodological and epistemic issues: 'meta-metaphysics'. He also works at the interface of metaphysics and philosophy of science: 'metaphysics of science'. Tahko is the author of *Unity of Science* (Cambridge University Press, 2021, *Elements in Philosophy of Science*), *An Introduction to Metametaphysics* (Cambridge University Press, 2015) and editor of *Contemporary Aristotelian Metaphysics* (Cambridge University Press, 2012).

About the series

This highly accessible series of Elements provides brief but comprehensive introductions to the most central topics in metaphysics. Many of the Elements also go into considerable depth, so the series will appeal to both students and academics. Some Elements bridge the gaps between metaphysics, philosophy of science, and epistemology.

Cambridge Elements ☰

Metaphysics

Elements in the series

Substance
Donnchadh O'Conaill

Essence
Martin Glazier

Truthmaking
Jamin Asay

Laws of Nature
Tyler Hildebrand

Dispositions and Powers
Toby Friend and Samuel Kimpton-Nye

Modality
Sònia Roca Royes

Parts and Wholes: Spatial to Modal
Meg Wallace

Indeterminacy in the World
Alessandro Torza

Parts and Wholes
Meg Wallace

Formal Ontology
Jani Hakkarainen, Markku Keinänen

Chemistry's Metaphysics
Vanessa A. Seifert

Ontological Categories: A Methodological Guide
Katarina Perović

A full series listing is available at: www.cambridge.org/EMPH

For EU product safety concerns, contact us at Calle de José Abascal, 56–1°, 28003 Madrid, Spain or eugpsr@cambridge.org.

www.ingramcontent.com/pod-product-compliance
Ingram Content Group UK Ltd.
Pitfield, Milton Keynes, MK11 3LW, UK
UKHW022144080726
473066UK00010B/751

* 9 7 8 1 1 0 8 9 7 8 2 5 5 *